SHW

T

The Attention Zone

A Parents' Guide to Attention Deficit/Hyperactivity Disorder

Michael W. Cohen, M.D.

BRUNNER/MAZEL
A member of the Taylor & Francis Group

USA	Publishing Office:	Taylor & Francis 1101 Vermont Avenue, N.W., Suite 200 Washington, DC 20005-3521 Tel: (202) 289-2174 Fax: (202) 289-3665
	Distribution Center:	Taylor & Francis 1900 Frost Road, Suite 101 Bristol, PA 19007-1598 Tel: (215) 785-5800 Fax: (215) 785-5515
UK		Taylor & Francis Ltd. 1 Gunpowder Square London EC4A 3DE Tel: 0171 583 0490 Fax: 0171 583 0581

THE ATTENTION ZONE: A Parents' Guide to Attention Deficit/ Hyperactivity Disorder

1 2 3 4 5 6 7 8 9 0   H P H P   9 0 9 8 7

This book was set in Times Roman. The editors were Greg Edmondson, Laura Haefner, and Alison Howson. Cover design by Michelle Fleitz.

A CIP catalog record for this book is available from the British Library.

∞ The paper in this publication meets the requirements of the ANSI Standard Z39.48-1984 (Permanence of Paper)

Library of Congress Cataloging-in-Publication Data

Cohen, Michael W., 1942–
    The attention zone: a parents' guide to attention deficit/hyperactivity disorder/ Michael Cohen.
    p. cm.

    1. Attention-deficit hyperactivity disorder—Popular works.
  I. Title.
RJ506.H9C625 1997   97-22972
618.92′8589—dc12   CIP

ISBN 0-87630-860-4 (paper)

Dedication

This book is dedicated to Susan, my wife, my best friend, the wonderful mother of our children, my lover and now business colleague. She has been extremely supportive throughout my professional career. I will forever cherish her love, companionship, and support. To my children, Jill, Greg, and new daughter Andrea, for being who they are, for their love and dedication to our family life.

Contents

Preface

For most adults, parenting children is a major focus of their life. For the parents of a child or adolescent with attention deficit/hyperactivity disorder (ADHD), this responsibility increases substantially because of the multiple roles they must play in order to be most helpful to their child. Parents are teachers, behavioral managers, coaches, maids, chauffeurs, their child's best friends and worst friends (at times), advocates, paralegals, students, disciplinarians, and confidantes. Parents of ADHD youngsters must assume these roles with consistency, positive energy, and an expenditure of enormous resources on almost a 24-hour-a-day basis.

Often, many professionals are involved in the identification, evaluation, and management of an ADHD youngster; however, the burden of responsibility for ensuring a youngster's success, as well as the vast majority of worry and concern, lies with the parents.

Education is an absolute necessity if parents are to assume their various roles successfully and ensure the best possible outcomes for their child. This book is dedicated to this self-education process for parents. Currently available knowledge regarding ADHD is presented, as well as treatment recommendations that have been shown to be useful for many youngsters and their families.

KIDS WHO ARE DIFFERENT

Here's to the kids who are different,
Kids who don't always get A's,
Kids who have ears
Twice the size of their peers,
And noses that go on for days,
Here's to the kids who are different,
Kids they call crazy or dumb,
Kids who don't fit,
With the guts and the grit,
Who dance to a different drum,
Here's to the kids who are different,
Kids with the mischievous streak,
For when they have grown,
As history has shown,
It's their difference that makes them unique.

—Digby Wolfe

1

So Many Questions

Many parents have concerns about how their child is doing in school and with friends. They also sense that raising their child is more difficult and challenging than they ever anticipated. All of a sudden someone—a neighbor, a relative, the teacher, or the principal—says: "I think your child has an attention disorder" or "I think your child is hyperactive." Parents differ a great deal in their reaction to such statements. Many parents deny the possibility; others get angry. Some accept the possibility but feel criticized as parents because of their possible role in causing the problems. Others have a sense that attention disorders are medical problems and that anybody who is not a doctor has no right drawing a conclusion. Some recognize the behavior problems and accept the attention disorder diagnosis but hope and pray that it will quickly get better without treatment. Other parents accept the possible diagnosis as a probable cause of their child's problems, want to learn as much as they can, and get started on improving the situation.

Regardless of the emotional reaction to the first mention of an attention disorder or hyperactivity, most parents initially or eventually have many questions about ADHD, how it might affect their child, and what they are supposed to do about it.

The questions, seemingly endless, can be separated into categories:

1. What is ADHD and why are we hearing so much about it?

2. Who should make the diagnosis, and what's involved?

3. What is the best way to treat ADHD?

4. What can we expect for the future?

As shown in the sections to follow, these categories involve numerous secondary questions as well.

WHAT IS ADHD AND WHY ARE WE HEARING SO MUCH ABOUT IT?

- Why is the disorder so much more prevalent now than ever before? Is it new?

- My child wants to be good but can't. Am I doing something wrong?

- My other kid is perfect. I've done the same thing with this one. Why isn't it working?

- My child seems so good at some things but gives up so easily on others. Why?

- Sometimes he can really pay attention; other times he doesn't. Why?

- Can't she just try harder?

- Why does he give up so quickly? The minute he feels he can't do something, he stops.

- I don't understand her explosions. She gets so upset she is out of control.

- Nothing seems to faze him. Even severe punishments don't work. Why?

- Why does only one kid in the family have this problem?

- If ADHD is a hereditary problem, why has no one in our family been diagnosed?

- Do food allergies cause ADHD?

- She seems to have no friends. Is this part of ADHD?

- I'm really worried about his self-esteem. He says such negative things about himself. Why does such a nice kid feel this way?

- She says she can't fall asleep. Is this part of ADHD, or does she just want to stay awake later?

■ Our life is a mess. Whenever he's at home, the family is in constant chaos. The other kids are suffering. What should I tell them?

■ She is so smart; why can't she learn?

■ The school says he can't have ADHD because he pays attention when he is interested. Is this true?

■ My family thinks I'm just a lousy parent. They don't believe she has ADHD. What can I say?

WHO SHOULD MAKE THE DIAGNOSIS, AND WHAT'S INVOLVED?

■ Is there a specific test for ADHD? How will I know if my child really has ADHD or just has a behavior problem?

■ I've been to my pediatrician. He says my daughter doesn't have attention disorder because she can watch TV and play video games. Is this true?

■ The school wants him to get medication before they test him. Is this right?

■ Some people say that the best way to diagnose ADHD is to try Ritalin and see if it helps. Is this a good idea?

■ Why do we have to fill out so many forms to evaluate our child for ADHD?

■ The school says they can make a diagnosis of ADHD. I thought only a doctor could make the diagnosis. Am I right?

■ What are the DSM criteria that I've heard about?

■ I've talked to three teachers, one doctor, the school psychologist, and a counselor, and they can't agree about whether my child has ADHD. Why is it so confusing?

WHAT IS THE BEST WAY TO TREAT ADHD?

■ The schools say they can't help me with my child's attention problem. Is that true?

- Why does everybody get Ritalin so quickly when people think they can't pay attention?

- What can I do to help? I'm really frightened of medication.

- Isn't there any other way to help other than medication?

- How long has this Ritalin medication been around?

- How will we know when we can stop the medication?

- What are the side effects of medication?

- I'm afraid putting him on medication will just postpone his learning how to take care of his problems by himself. Is this true?

- I've heard that changing a youngster's diet or giving vitamins can help with hyperactivity and attention problems. Is this true?

- The school is always calling me to come pick him up because of his disruptive behavior. Isn't there anything they can do with him?

- The teacher says she doesn't have time with 32 kids to help my child. Isn't that her job?

- Homework time is outrageous. It is a constant struggle. What can we do?

- He wants to play Little League, but the coach says he just doesn't fit in. What activities would be good for him?

- Is her current school the right place? It is so big and seems impersonal.

- The school won't help him because they say he is not trying. I think he's not trying because he can't be successful. What do you think?

- When she misses a dose of medicine, she blames her problems on not getting her medicine. I think she is growing dependent on it. Is she manipulating us?

- My nephew took Ritalin and it worked perfectly. Why isn't it helping my son?

- There is a lot of addiction in my family. I'm really frightened of the medication. Can she become addicted to it, or can it lead to other drug abuse?

- I want to say nice things to him and reward him, but it is so hard to find anything that he does right. Where do I start?

- Every time we try something new with her, it just helps for a little while. It seems that she outgrows all the medication and our behavioral strategies. Why is this?

- It sounds like you want me to be a therapist for my child all day every day. Is that what you mean?

WHAT CAN WE EXPECT FOR THE FUTURE?

- She is using ADHD as an excuse. Now she says she can't do anything. What should I do?

- He used to take his medicine so well. Now that he is 12, he is refusing. What can we do?

- She was doing so well, and all of a sudden she seems really depressed. She is withdrawing from her friends. Could the medicine have caused this?

- Why does he resist our efforts to help him so much?

- We're doing all the things that you told us, but she seems only a little bit better. How will we know if we are doing enough?

- Is it true that most kids with ADHD have problems as adults?

- I've heard that ADHD kids wind up being depressed. Is this true?

- Once ADHD is on his school records, won't the school give up on him?

- Is it true that you can't go in the military if you have ADHD?

- Is there a lot of job discrimination for people with ADHD?

- If he is so difficult now, what will he be like when he's 15 years old?

- How long will she need to be on medication?

This is only a sample of the enormous number of questions raised for all parents confronted with the mention of attention disorder or hyperactivity either initially or as they progress through an evaluation or treatment. The remaining chapters are dedicated to answering as many of these questions as possible. It is important to remember, as emphasized throughout this book, that **people with ADHD are more different than they are alike.** The symptoms and needs of every individual are different, but once these differences are understood, effective treatment is available for ADHD.

2

Introduction:
The Core Symptoms

ADHD is currently the most common behavioral disturbance diagnosed among children and adolescents in the United States. The symptoms displayed by youngsters with this diagnosis vary tremendously, however. The expression of this developmental disorder depends to a great extent on other characteristics of the individual. This chapter reviews the various behaviors associated with the core symptoms of ADHD: hyperactivity, inattention, distractibility, impulsivity, and an excessive need for attention. The formal criteria for ADHD are presented. The symptoms commonly associated with ADHD are discussed in depth to provide a full appreciation of the possible profile of an individual with this diagnosis.

The behaviors that represent core symptoms vary significantly from person to person. These differences may depend on:

1. The severity of a youngster's symptomatology

2. The youngster's temperament or personality

3. The youngster's profile of other developmental strengths and weaknesses

4. The youngster's life experiences, both within and outside the family

5. The youngster's level of emotional comfort resulting from his or her life successes and disappointments

6. The messages the youngster has received from peers and adults regarding his or her competency

7. The youngster's ability to be successful in various areas of life

8. The youngster's age

Approximately 3% to 6% of all American school-aged children are currently diagnosed as having ADHD. This rate exceeds that of individuals diagnosed as having ADHD in other countries. The reason for this difference is not clear. Some professionals believe that we are overdiagnosing the problem in the United States, while others perceive that professionals elsewhere are not adequately diagnosing individuals with more subtle forms of the disorder. Many people ask whether this condition existed in previous generations. In fact, when a careful history is obtained from families with ADHD youngsters, almost invariably some family member had a similar profile during his or her youth but was not specifically diagnosed or treated. In addition, other family members may have been diagnosed as having developmental disorders that frequently coexist with ADHD (for example, learning disabilities) but may have had minimal ADHD symptoms. The tendency toward these types of disorders is hereditary but not necessarily specific to the symptoms of a given individual. Hereditary factors, discussed in Chapter 4, are clearly the most powerful predictors of ADHD.

SEX AND AGE FACTORS

Many research studies have reported that for each girl diagnosed with ADHD, six to eight boys will be diagnosed. Clinicians believe that the reason females of all ages with ADHD are significantly underdiagnosed is that, as a result of their generally less severe behavior problems, they do not bring attention to themselves. Some studies have shown that similar symptoms exist in boys and girls but that boys' symptoms are quantitatively more severe. This is especially true in regard to aggression, oppositional behaviors, and externalizing behaviors. Girls may, however, have learning disabilities, language disorders, and mood disturbances that are as severe as, if not more severe than, the corresponding symptoms in their male counterparts. The true male-to-female ratio of individuals with ADHD is therefore unknown. There has been some suggestion that separate diagnostic criteria be developed for males and females. This issue is quite controversial, since no such differences exist for other behavioral or developmental disturbances.

ADHD has long been considered a disorder of childhood and adolescence, with the assumption that most teenagers outgrow their symptoms sometime during their middle teenage years. It is now clear that ADHD is potentially a life-span disorder. Approximately 80% of children will continue to have symptoms into their adolescent years; the number of adults who continue to have symptoms is unknown. The reason for this lack of information is the recent dramatic increase in the diagnosis of attention disorders among adults.

It is unclear why some individuals outgrow their symptoms while others continue to have attention disorder characteristics. It is not believed that adequate and appropriate intervention in childhood or adolescence automatically precludes the possibility of adult symptoms. Some professionals speculate that, as is the case with other medical conditions, there are family patterns of this biological disorder. For example, asthma and diabetes often have typical family profiles in terms of onset and course of illness. ADHD symptoms may be determined by these familial patterns. The challenge to parents, therefore, is to prepare their children and adolescents by helping them build up as much self-confidence as possible as they enter their adult years. Assisting a teenager in developing adequate coping strategies, insight into his or her strengths and limitations, and positive self-esteem are the outcome goals. These goals are necessary since parents and professionals do not have control of the biological pattern or persistence of symptoms for any individual child.

THE CORE SYMPTOMS

The core symptoms of ADHD are typically described as hyperactivity, inattention, distractibility, and impulsivity. Many parents would include a fifth core symptom: excessive need for attention. The quality, intensity, and severity of these core symptoms differ enormously from one individual to another. They also may differ substantially from one situation to another. This unevenness in symptoms at different times and in different situations is typical of many individuals with ADHD. For example, many youngsters' symptoms are worse in a busy, stimulating classroom than in a relatively quiet, calm, and unstimulating home environment. Some children with ADHD will do much better with one type of teacher than another. A youngster with a teacher who maintains a relatively calm atmosphere, is structured, defines his or her expectations for students, and provides a great deal of positive reinforcement may exhibit considerably better self-control, appropriate behavior, and improved performance.

Various stresses tend to accentuate ADHD core symptoms. These stresses include:

- A high level of environmental stimulation

- Fatigue

- Previous lack of success in a particular situation

- Emotional stress

- Unanticipated changes in routine (and thus expectations)

- Excessive fear regarding consequences of behaviors

- In some youngsters, an excess of intake of refined sugars

These factors, among others, often contribute to the appearance of unevenness in the behavioral and performance profile of a youngster with ADHD. Such unevenness (doing well in some situations and circumstances and poorly in others) often leads to the rejection of ADHD as a possible diagnosis and to the conclusion that emotional factors are the primary cause of a child's difficulty. By definition, ADHD symptoms must be present across two of the three typical areas—school, home, and with peers—of a youngster's life. There may, however, be a selective nature or inconsistency present in a child's ability to self-regulate and meet adult expectations. For example, the diagnosis of ADHD is often excluded as a consideration if a youngster can watch TV relatively quietly or play a video game. Watching TV is such a passive exercise that it demands very little active attention. Video games provide the ideal stimulation for a child with attentional difficulties. The child has full control and can change the visual field as soon as he or she becomes inattentive or disinterested. In addition, most youngsters are not judged by their video game performance, and they have freedom of play without the criticism often associated with other activities and responsibilities.

In considering a diagnosis of ADHD, it is also important to recognize that, at times, all children exhibit symptoms typically associated with this diagnosis. Some children are innately more active than others. Many children exhibit fleeting attention when they are highly stimulated or excited. Other children are impulsive before they learn caution. The key to considering ADHD is whether the child has age-appropriate behavioral regulation skills in situations that require self-control. A very active child may be fine if she or he is able to sit still, attend properly, and complete tasks in a classroom situation or other situations requiring this level of control. Another diagnostic criteria is the persistence of symptoms over time. While the symptoms may change as a youngster gets older, those appropriately diagnosed with ADHD will evidence a certain degree of persistence, in terms of symptoms, across many situations.

Hyperactivity

The symptoms of hyperactivity generally change with age. Young children are often motorically active, running instead of walking and frequently appearing to be internally driven. They are unable to engage in any activity for a sustained period of time and generally move from one thing to another without any significant involvement. Some youngsters are simply fidgety. They are able to remain in their seat at dinner but are constantly fidgeting, moving one body part or another and often even distracting themselves. Other youngsters are verbally hyperactive, speaking rapidly and incessantly, often without having any specific purpose or making any point. Hyperactivity tends to lessen with age, evolving to fidgety behavior and eventually to only intermittent motoric excesses. Teenagers may be overly active only in the face of stress.

Hyperactivity tends to be the most disruptive ADHD characteristic, especially in a classroom situation. Hyperactive youngsters are often not aware of the extent to which their activity level disrupts others, and they deny their symptoms when questioned. Hyperactivity is not a necessary feature of ADHD. Many individuals with ADHD have only an inattentive type with no evidence of excess motor activity.

Inattention and Distractibility

Youngsters with ADHD often have great difficulty sustaining their attention to a given task, whether it be academic or recreational. They are typically bored easily by activities that don't greatly interest them. They often don't appear to be listening. Those with specific auditory attention difficulties are often labeled as having behavioral problems because of their noncompliance. In fact, they were never listening carefully enough to understand the directions. They may be highly motivated to complete tasks as directed, but distractions often divert them in a different direction. They may be distracted through excessive attention to irrelevant stimuli. In a classroom situation, an ADHD student might be distracted by the activities of others, a subtle flickering of a fluorescent lightbulb, or even the holes in the ceiling tiles. When asked, many youngsters will acknowledge that they are internally distracted by their own thoughts. These thoughts are often intrusive and interrupt their ability to maintain attention and complete tasks. Such thoughts may relate to past or future recreational activities or simply imaginative daydreaming. Some youngsters will be distracted by persistent worries and be unable to attend to classroom activities. Many youngsters with attention disorders have great difficulty organizing and prioritizing their approach to a task. They are often overwhelmed by a multistage task or academic assignment. They often seem to have no appreciation for the benefits of maintaining order in their academic, home, or play lives. In many instances, they can initiate attention but not sustain it adequately to complete tasks. Many older youngsters with ADHD will dedicate themselves to maintaining appropriate attention and avoiding distractions in order to complete tasks. These individuals may reach their goals briefly but often burn out because of the extra effort necessary to maintain their attention and complete tasks.

It is a misconception that individuals with inattention and distractibility are unable to pay attention. If their motivation is significantly elevated because the task is of particular interest, youngsters with ADHD may well initiate adequate attention and even maintain it for some period of time. Unfortunately, the effort and motivation required are difficult to sustain over time, the individual's effort often gradually deteriorating despite his or her best intent. Thus, the issue, in terms of inattention and distractibility, is not necessarily the individual's lack of capability in these areas but the amount of motivation and energy required to initiate attention, avoid distractions, and sustain effort.

Impulsivity

Youngsters with impulsivity as one of their core symptoms often respond to a situation without considering the inappropriateness or consequences of their actions. Such children may place themselves in danger by impulsively leaving parents, running in the street, or attempting tasks beyond their ability. In the school setting, they may yell out an answer before being called upon, show poor judgment in decision making, be unable to wait their turn in games or school routines, or need immediate gratification for their desires. They are often labeled as aggressive in classroom situations because of their reflexive overreaction. Such overreaction stems from their inability to delay their response long enough to interpret the social cues of a given situation. Impulsive teenagers often put themselves or others in danger or behave in a socially inappropriate manner in an attempt to gain peer acceptance or to be noticed. They also may exhibit impulsively antisocial behavior as a result of anger and alienation stemming from a lack of social and academic success.

Most youngsters with ADHD can intellectually recognize the inappropriateness of their actions and are often remorseful. Unfortunately, their awareness of how to behave does not always translate to their performing appropriately because of their impulsivity. Impulsivity often leads to youngsters being labeled as having behavioral problems, as being disrespectful and rude, and as not caring about the feelings of others. In fact, many impulsive youngsters are deeply sensitive and as upset about their behaviors as the people judging them. They simply lack the ability to delay or postpone their actions long enough to consider consequences and inhibit their responses.

Excessive Need for Attention

Many ADHD youngsters have difficulty delaying their desire for gratification. They want what they want when they want it. They are also often quite persistent until they feel gratified. Many have an insatiable desire for attention and are intolerant of anybody or anything that competes for that attention. Many parents indicate that if they spent their entire day on a one-to-one basis attempting to satisfy the needs of their child with ADHD, they would still fall short. This symptom is closely related to impulsivity in that children are unable to achieve gratification on a delayed basis. If youngsters with ADHD experience a lack of success socially or academically, their need for attention may escalate.

DIAGNOSTIC CRITERIA

The current formal diagnostic criteria for ADHD are defined by the American Psychiatric Association in the fourth edition of the *Diagnostic and Statistical Manual of Mental Disorders* (DSM-IV). ADHD is divided into three major categories:

- Predominantly Inattentive
- Predominantly Hyperactive-Impulsive
- Combined

These criteria (see Table 1) describe the core symptoms of ADHD well. To meet the criteria for diagnosis, a youngster must (a) have a certain number of characteristics in each category to define his or her type of ADHD, (b) have symptoms by age 7, (c) exhibit symptoms significant enough to impair function in at least two of three settings (school, home, and with peers), and (d) not have other significant emotional or medical disorders as causes of symptoms.

Table 1
Diagnostic Criteria for ADHD

A. Either (1) or (2)
    (1) six (or more) of the following symptoms of inattention have persisted for at least 6 months to a degree that is maladaptive and inconsistent with developmental level:
    Inattention
        (a) often fails to give close attention to details or makes careless mistakes in school-work, work, or other activities
        (b) often has difficulty sustaining attention in tasks or play activities
        (c) often does not seem to listen when spoken to directly
        (d) often does not follow through on instructions and fails to finish schoolwork, chores, or duties in the workplace (not due to oppositional behavior or failure to understand directions)
        (e) often has difficulty organizing tasks and activities
        (f) often avoids, dislikes, or is reluctant to engage in tasks that require sustained mental effort (such as schoolwork or homework)
        (g) often loses things necessary for tasks or activities (e.g., toys, school assignments, pencils, books, or tools)
        (h) is often easily distracted by extraneous stimuli
        (i) is often forgetful in daily activities

    (2) six (or more) of the following symptoms of hyperactivity-impulsivity have persisted for at least 6 months to a degree that is maladaptive and inconsistent with developmental level:

    Hyperactivity
        (a) often fidgets with hands or feet or squirms in seat
        (b) often leaves seat in classroom or in other situations in which remaining seated is expected
        (c) often runs about or climbs excessively in situations in which it is inappropriate (in adolescents or adults, may be limited to subjective feelings of restlessness)
        (d) often has difficulty playing or engaging in leisure activities quietly
        (e) is often "on the go" or often acts as if "driven by a motor"
        (f) often talks excessively

    Impulsivity
        (g) often blurts out answers before questions have been completed
        (h) often has difficulty awaiting turn
        (i) often interrupts or intrudes on others (e.g., butts into conversations or games)
B. Some hyperactive-impulsive or inattentive symptoms that caused impairment were present before age 7 years
C. Some impairment from the symptoms is present in two or more settings (e.g., at school [or work] and at home).
D. There must be clear evidence of clinically significant impairment in social, academic, or occupational functioning.
E. The symptoms do not occur exclusively during the course of a pervasive developmental disorder, schizophrenia, or other psychotic disorder and are not better accounted for by another mental disorder (e.g., mood disorder, anxiety disorder, dissociative disorder, or personality disorder).

Table 1
Diagnostic Criteria for ADHD (*Continued*)

Code based on type:

314.01 Attention-Deficit/Hyperactivity Disorder. Combined Type: if both Criteria A1 and A2 are met for the past 6 months

314.00 Attention-Deficit/Hyperactivity Disorder. Predominantly Inattentive Type: if Criterion A1 is met but Criterion A2 is not met for the past 6 months

314.01 Attention-Deficit/Hyperactivity Disorder. Predominantly Hyperactive-Impulsive Type: if Criterion A2 is met but Criterion A1 is not met for the past 6 months

---

Note. For individuals (especially adolescents and adults) who currently have symptoms that no longer meet full criteria, "in partial remission" should be specified. DSM-IV, American Psychiatric Association, 1994.

In the DSM-IV system, numbers are assigned to each diagnosis. These numbers are used as a shorthand communication for official clinical or administrative documents. For ADHD, the assigned numbers are as follows:

ADHD, Inattentive Type: 314.00
ADHD, Impulsive-Hyperactive Type: 314.01
ADHD, Combined Type: 314.01

While the purpose of these criteria is to help professionals gain a perspective of ADHD and to allow for communication among clinicians, the criteria should not be used as an exclusive diagnostic test. Simply confirming that a youngster has enough of the stated characteristics to qualify for the ADHD diagnosis may be misleading in terms of the actual cause of these symptoms and may be too limited, considering the broad spectrum of symptoms associated with the ADHD label. In addition, other behavioral disturbances share many symptoms with ADHD. Remember, individuals with ADHD are much more different than they are alike.

3

The Full ADHD Symptom Profile: Coexisting Conditions

A variety of developmental, behavioral, and medical conditions exist so frequently in association with ADHD core symptoms that they must be considered an integral part of this syndrome. In conjunction with the core symptoms, these difficulties and conditions define the full profile of ADHD in children and adolescents. A knowledge of this profile is essential to understanding ADHD and the needs of individuals diagnosed with the condition. Treatment success, in both the short and the long term, will depend on transforming these needs into an effective individualized program.

COEXISTING SYMPTOMS

Figure 1 displays the full profile of possible symptoms for ADHD children and adolescents. The core ADHD symptoms are in the center, surrounded by coexisting symptoms. The left side of the chart indicates the associated developmental, medical, and learning problems; the right side indicates common behavioral and emotional disturbances. The percentages under each condition are estimates of the prevalence of these diagnoses and symptoms in individuals with ADHD. These percentages are based on research studies and may vary substantially based on the setting (i.e., school versus psychiatric clinic) in which the diagnosis is considered and the age of the individual.

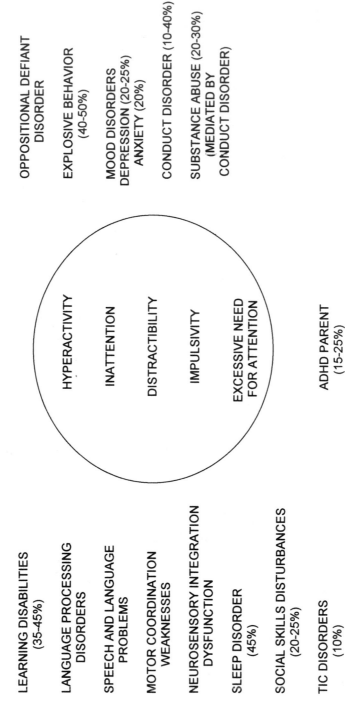

STRENGTHS
(100%)

OPPOSITIONAL DEFIANT
DISORDER

EXPLOSIVE BEHAVIOR
(40-50%)

MOOD DISORDERS
DEPRESSION (20-25%)
ANXIETY (20%)

CONDUCT DISORDER (10-40%)

SUBSTANCE ABUSE (20-30%)
(MEDIATED BY
CONDUCT DISORDER)

HYPERACTIVITY

INATTENTION

DISTRACTIBILITY

IMPULSIVITY

EXCESSIVE NEED
FOR ATTENTION

ADHD PARENT
(15-25%)

LEARNING DISABILITIES
(35-45%)

LANGUAGE PROCESSING
DISORDERS

SPEECH AND LANGUAGE
PROBLEMS

MOTOR COORDINATION
WEAKNESSES

NEUROSENSORY INTEGRATION
DYSFUNCTION

SLEEP DISORDER
(45%)

SOCIAL SKILLS DISTURBANCES
(20-25%)

TIC DISORDERS
(10%)

Figure 1
The Profile of ADHD Children and Adolescents

This chapter briefly describes the major coexisting symptoms and conditions, which are listed subsequently.

1. Strengths

2. Learning disabilities, such as dyslexia

3. Language processing disorders

4. Mild to moderate speech delays and articulation problems

5. Fine and gross motor incoordination

6. Sleep disorders

7. Tic disorders

8. Social skills disturbances

9. Oppositional behavior disorders

10. Explosive behavior

11. Mood disorders, such as anxiety and depression

12. Conduct or antisocial problems with and without substance abuse

Strengths

Understanding the strengths of every child or adolescent is as essential as an awareness of their needs and is particularly important in developing an intervention program. Unfortunately, most evaluations overly focus on an individual's weaknesses without taking into account his or her personal resources. **All individuals with ADHD have strengths.** Understanding these resources or strengths is essential to the creation of a productive treatment program. For example, academically underachieving students may be quite intelligent even though their performance is lacking in terms of traditional measures of academic success. Creative children may be labeled as daydreamers or as lazy because their imagination interferes with their ability to produce. Some youngsters can be great problem solvers for others but cannot deal effectively with their own situation. Emotional qualities, such as being affectionate, caring for the feelings and needs of others, being loving, and desiring to share, are often overlooked during evaluations.

Many parents become quite resentful and discouraged when they sit in an office or at school staffings and hear nothing but the negative characteristics of their child, knowing that their child has many strengths and qualities unrecognized by the "evaluation team." The success of most intervention programs will depend on supporting youngsters' emotional needs by encouraging activities that highlight strengths and using these strengths to support weaknesses.

Learning Disabilities

Learning disabilities reflect an individual's inability to learn in an age-appropriate fashion despite having adequate ability (typically measured by intelligence tests). This discrepancy reflects an inefficiency or disorder in processing and retention of information received by the central nervous system (brain). Such processing disorders may relate to interpretation of information, memory, lack of ability to retrieve relevant information, or inability to use learned information for the performance of academic tasks. These weaknesses can be global or limited to reading (either sounding out words or comprehension), spelling, mathematics, or written language. Deficits in any of these areas will affect accomplishment in all related school subject areas.

Administratively, schools define learning disabilities as numerical or statistical discrepancies between measured IQ and academic performance on a 1:1 test of reading, mathematics, and written language skills or by the presence of a processing deficit. These discrepancy criteria are often defined by school district administrative and funding bodies based on the resources available and the number of students who can be served.

Studies show that learning disabilities coexist with ADHD anywhere from 10% to 90% of the time. It is reasonable to conclude that an ADHD youngster has a 35% to 45% chance of having a learning disability. Youngsters with learning disabilities have the same probability of having ADHD, even though the symptoms may be only subtle attention weaknesses or distractibility.

Language Processing Disorders

Language processing disorders represent a specific type of learning disability involving difficulty in processing oral language. *Receptive language processing disorders* exist when an individual hears adequately, knows the vocabulary, and may exhibit reasonable attention levels but does not "get" the message or idea being communicated. These youngsters typically will respond with answers unrelated to the topic being discussed. They also may have difficulties hearing the differences between similar words, remembering what they heard, and understanding vocabulary and concept words or grammatical forms. They may appear to be noncompliant because they never really understood what was being requested. Individuals with receptive language difficulties may be labeled as being lazy or as having a behavioral problem because of their noncompliance or their talking to another student to clarify directions. They may also develop an attention problem in that they pay less and less attention to oral language over time since it has minimal meaning for them.

Expressive language processing disorders are seen in youngsters who cannot retrieve words from their memory adequately to name or define things in daily speech. They also have difficulty formulating smooth, flowing ideas precisely, completely, and clearly in order to communicate in properly formed, age-appropriate sentences. They may have difficulty with pronouns, temporal relationships, possessives, or other rules of syntax. They often ramble on with stories, missing relevant details or never getting to the point.

There are enormous social and psychological consequences of language processing disorders. Mislabeling of a youngster with receptive difficulties as lazy often leads to anger and alienation, and the child may ultimately give up or act out. Expressive difficulties sensitize children to their inability to be understood, often leading to an unwillingness to attempt oral communication or behavioral problems in response to frustration. Evaluation and treatment of language processing disorders require the skills of an experienced speech and language professional.

The incidence of language processing disorders within a population of youth with ADHD is not specifically known. One study indicates that as many as one third of children with ADHD will have symptoms of a receptive language impairment and that two thirds will have an expressive language impairment. All of these children do not have a true language processing disorder; the majority of them ultimately developed what were believed to be functional speech and language capabilities. Their difficulty with impulse control and attention prevents them from using their skills to communicate effectively.

Speech and Language Delays

Basic speech and language delays and difficulties occur more commonly in individuals with ADHD than in the general population. These difficulties include delays in the initial onset or production of speech, articulation or pronunciation problems, and stuttering.

Motor Incoordination

Motor coordination weaknesses, in terms of both gross and fine motor skills, occur frequently with ADHD. Many youngsters lack gross motor skills and quickly lose interest in recreational or sports activities. In team sports, they may be the victims of teasing or criticism by teammates who are disappointed by their contributions to the team effort. Uninformed coaches often aggravate the situation as a result of their "style" (confrontation or criticism) of encouragement or teaching. Fine motor skills are especially relevant for the penmanship skills required early in a child's school career. Weaknesses in this area often limit "success" as measured by traditional grading approaches. The content of an assignment may be correct, but if the penmanship is illegible, the grade will often be reduced. The discouraging impact on a child's future writing efforts is obvious. Despite their writing difficulties, many youngsters with ADHD are excellent artists. In fact, they can be quite precise in terms of detail and may become overly focused on their art instead of completing their schoolwork.

Neurosensory Integration Dysfunction

Neurosensory integration dysfunction has been described by researchers in the field of occupational therapy. Youngsters exhibiting the appropriate characteristics for this diagnosis are not able to tolerate various sensations or stimuli. They typically involuntarily flap or clap their hands when excited or upset; show extreme physical tension when upset; are quite bothered by loud sounds or bright lights; are selective about who can touch them and when and how they can be touched; complain about clothing being uncomfortable or too tight; are picky eaters because of textures of foods; lose control of their behavior when highly stimulated; demonstrate self-stimulating behavior such as rocking, twirling in circles, or pacing aimlessly; have poor gross and fine motor coordination; and are hyperactive. Occupational therapists believe that these symptoms are caused by a dysfunction of the inner ear that also results in balance control problems. Many physicians do not accept this explanation and reject the existence of the diagnosis. Others have seen substantial benefit in the therapies used to treat these symptoms, which often involve rolling the child on therapy balls, rotational movements on swings, and brushing the skin.

Sleep Disorders

Sleep disorders occur in approximately 45% of children with ADHD. The most common complaint is an inability to relax and fall asleep. This symptom has great impact on the parent-child relationship because of the child's presumed active resistance to going to sleep. A late sleep time and inadequate sleep often lead to daytime fatigue and a reduction in the physical and mental stamina needed for adequate school performance and behavioral regulation and control. Other sleep problems, such as early (at times, very early) awakening, frequent waking during the night, and difficulty awakening in the morning and getting started for the day, occur more commonly in ADHD children. The implications of inadequate rest for the daytime functioning of ADHD youngsters are considerable. The treatment of this aspect of an ADHD child's life is often inadequately considered as the overall management program is developed and implemented. In fact, sleep problems may be further aggravated by medical interventions with stimulant medications and tolerated because of daytime improvements. Various behavioral and medical treatments can improve sleeping habits.

Tic Disorders

Tic disorders occur in approximately 10% of all individuals with ADHD. Motor tics are involuntary muscle movements such as eye blinking, facial grimacing, or head and shoulder shakes. Tic disorders may include gestures and habits such as having hands and fingers around the mouth and nose, picking at skin, picking at fingernails and nail beds, running fingers through the hair, and chewing on clothing. Vocal tics include involuntary throat clearing, grunting, snorting, sniffing, or sudden noise making for no apparent reason. Several types of tic disorders can occur with ADHD. Benign tic disorders of childhood represent a family pattern of temporary motor tics that come and go but are outgrown with age. Chronic tic disorders involve motor tics that wax and wane but are generally considered a lifelong disturbance. Gilles de la Tourette's syndrome involves both motor and vocal tics and is also a lifelong disorder. Chronic tic disorder and Tourette's syndrome are now considered to be the same condition with symptoms being on a broad spectrum of severity, and with Tourette's being most severe. Both are associated with a variety of behavioral disturbances, including obsessive-compulsive thinking, ritualistic behavior, unusual fears and phobias, verbal outbursts and destructive behavioral outbursts, and a general need for sameness.

Approximately 50% to 60% of individuals with this spectrum of chronic tic disorders will have an attentional disorder that is identical to and indistinguishable from ADHD, often being present before the onset of tics. Some treatments for ADHD, particularly the use of stimulant drugs, may allow tics to emerge earlier in an individual with a tic disorder than otherwise might have been the case. Other behavioral symptoms of tic disorders can be accentuated despite the attentional benefits of these medications.

Social Skills Disturbances

A variety of social skills disturbances, such as blurting out answers to questions, interrupting or intruding on the conversations of others, failing to notice or tend to important social cues, and handling frustration in an impulsive, aggressive manner, commonly occur with ADHD. Additional social deficits include failing to comprehend the impact of one's actions on others, misinterpreting social information, failing to understand social boundaries, and having difficulty monitoring and reacting to the ongoing stream of social interactions. Many youngsters with ADHD are bossy and attempt to be in control of all social situations. They often are excluded from age-appropriate social activities such as birthday parties. They commonly complain that no one likes them, or they project blame onto others for problems they created. These symptoms may create a social disability in approximately 20% to 25% of individuals with ADHD. The severity of these symptoms and their impact on daily life differ tremendously among ADHD youngsters. Many youngsters with ADHD have significant strengths in terms of social interaction and evolve as leaders among their peers.

Oppositional Behavior Disorders

Oppositional defiant disorder is generally considered a psychologically based behavioral disturbance that coexists with ADHD approximately 40% to 50% of the time, especially in preschool-aged and young school-aged children. These youngsters are extremely resistant to adult requests and oppose whatever people desire of them. (These symptoms may be seen even in preverbal children.) Children will often say "I'm not doing that, and you can't make me." They often persist relentlessly in their resistance and protest. Tantrums may occur, even over trivial issues. These tantrums are severe and occur almost reflexively, before the child has an opportunity to deliberate and process the request.

Explosive Behavior

Behavioral explosiveness occurs often with ADHD core symptoms and is considered by some clinicians as a subtype of ADHD. The major feature is reflexive, severe, negative behavioral overreactivity. Episodes or spells usually begin abruptly and involve a severe verbal or destructive reaction, often to a minor incident. Typically, parents describe their child as appearing to be out of control and at times frightening. The spells often escalate as parents attempt to intervene. Resolution of the outburst often requires placing the child (or the child placing herself or himself) in a quiet, nonstimulating situation that allows her or him to "settle down." After the spell, the child may often be remorseful. In addition to the outbursts, these youngsters may be aggressive with peers and perhaps adults. As well, they may have little tolerance for change or for being told "no" when they desire to do or have something. They are often also extremely impulsive.

Mood Disorders

Mood disorders can occur in children and adolescents with symptoms that may be similar to those of adults. Youngsters with depression may appear sad; have feelings of helplessness, hopelessness, or worthlessness; be self-critical; exhibit a loss of interest in activities; have low self-esteem and excessive guilt; evidence a change in sleep patterns and be fatigued; and show loss of appetite and energy. Since children often lack sufficient insight as to their feelings or the vocabulary to express their feelings, their depression may be expressed behaviorally. They may appear angry, cry excessively, become aggressive, have physical complaints, express fears or anxieties, isolate themselves, or exhibit a progressive drop in school performance or interest in peer and family interaction. For an ADHD population, these symptoms tend to occur in older adolescents or young adults but can occur at any age. This diagnosis must be considered in younger individuals as well when their performance deteriorates rapidly or significantly. Overall, 20% to 25% of ADHD individuals (of all ages) will experience depression.

Anxiety disorders occur in approximately 20% of ADHD individuals. Anxiety disorders in children can take many forms, including separation anxiety from parents, unusual or accentuated fears and phobias, excessive worries about the safety and welfare of family members and friends, and an intense anxiety about school performance (to the point at which performance actually worsens). Most children have normal fears of the dark, of monsters, or of being alone. Over time, these normal fears usually fade. However, when they persist and become magnified or when they interfere with a child's normal daily routine, the diagnosis of anxiety disorder may be appropriate.

Conduct or Antisocial Problems

Conduct disorders involve socially unacceptable behaviors such as stealing, fire setting, truancy, property destruction, robbery or burglary, aggression, physical cruelty to animals, use of a weapon to hurt or intimidate others, and forcing another into sexual activity. These symptoms typically begin in early or midadolescence but may be seen in childhood. The diagnosis requires persistent patterns of behavior rather than a single or rare event. Conduct disorders are seen in 10% to 40% of ADHD individuals.

Substance Abuse

Substance abuse, on an experimental basis, occurs commonly in the teenage population. Chronic substance abuse is more likely in adolescents with ADHD than in the general population only if these adolescents have engaged in conduct disorder behavior. However, the impulsivity associated with ADHD may lead to some increase in experimentation. Many clinicians believe that older teenagers and young adults with undiagnosed or untreated ADHD use substances in an attempt to self-medicate for relief of their various symptoms. Nicotine is used commonly because it may have a stimulation effect that benefits ADHD individuals by relieving the stressful feelings associated with the frustrations of daily life.

SUMMARY

For each child or adolescent diagnosed with ADHD, there is a 15% to 25% probability that one of his or her parents will have **adult ADHD**. This parent may or may not have been diagnosed as having ADHD as a child and may have retained some of the characteristics in adulthood. Most clinicians see many parents who "self-diagnose" themselves during the evaluation of their children. Many ADHD parents find that they are better prepared to meet the challenges of treating their ADHD youngsters when they themselves have been effectively treated. Since the symptoms of adults with ADHD can be caused by several medical and psychological conditions, an experienced professional is required to diagnose and treat these individuals.

Because of this broad spectrum of possible coexisting symptoms, youngsters with ADHD are truly much more different than they are alike, perhaps having only one of the core symptoms in common. An understanding of these profiles, in addition to the youngster's strengths, resilience, and capacity for social and academic learning, is an essential ingredient of evaluation and individualized treatment programs.

4

What Causes ADHD:
The Attention Zone

A ttention disorders involve a number of causes. ADHD is one—and probably the most common—cause of symptoms. Clearly, the most powerful predictor of ADHD is a positive family history of similar symptoms and other developmental delays. As previously shown in Figure 1, for each youngster with ADHD, there is a 15% to 25% probability that one of his or her parents will also have ADHD. This hereditary profile is often discovered through a careful history of the lives of family members with similar symptoms. Within families with ADHD individuals, the ADHD symptoms of various members may be quite different from those of the child or adolescent who is having difficulty.

These hereditary influences seem to cause a variation in the biochemistry of one or several areas of the nervous system. The specific biochemical difference has not yet been fully proven. Even though there is probably more than one biochemical variation leading to these symptoms, there is a common theme in the medical research. There seems to be an inadequate amount of chemicals called neurotransmitters between brain cells in the area of the brain responsible for behavioral and motor regulation. Neurotransmitters connect brain cells and serve as the wiring or circuitry of the brain. Brain cells connected by neurotransmitters create patterns that allow information to be processed. An inadequacy in these chemicals causes a slowing or inefficiency in the processing or sorting of information. Behavioral regulation requires a rapid, accurate processing of information from the environment. For example, while attempting to pay attention, an individual must instantaneously—almost reflexively—identify and label a potential distraction, decide not to respond, and then actively inhibit his or her reaction in order to effectively sustain attention. Distractions may be internal (one's own thoughts) or external (environmental activity). If transmitters are inadequate, information is processed too slowly, not allowing for effective inhibition or regulation of behavioral responses. Slow processing of information results in the distraction intruding into the individual's attention, with a loss of the opportunity to maintain attention. The same scenario is true for hyperactivity, with a child requiring an active inhibition of movement in order to sit still. The child is moving before she or he can appreciate the necessity of sitting still and impose a movement inhibition on herself or himself. Impulsivity control requires an efficient consideration of the consequences of an impulse and a rapid inhibition of one's response. Slow processing does not allow for this active inhibition, resulting in uncontrolled, impulsive responses, often with remorse after consequences occur.

Figures 2 through 4 portray the complicated interactions between the ability to pay attention and adequate neurotransmitter levels (as in ADHD), motivation/effort, emotional comfort, and stamina. While ADHD has focused on the neurotransmitter issue, day-to-day behavioral regulation, including paying attention, reflects many human characteristics and is a complicated process. **Motivation and effort** are clearly determining factors. Many individuals conceptually desire to do well but are unable to or unwilling to make the effort necessary to accomplish the tasks required to achieve that success. Both are necessary for consistent attention.

The ability to attend is relative; even the most affected ADHD individual is able to attend if his or her motivation and effort are significantly elevated on a temporary basis. The issue for most ADHD individuals, then, is how hard they have to work to gain attention and then how long they can sustain this effort.

Stamina refers to the physical energy necessary to maintain attention. Stamina is enhanced by (a) good physical health, (b) balanced nutrition, (c) the absence of chronic illness, (d) the absence of adverse medication effects, and (e) adequate sleep and rest.

Emotional comfort is absolutely necessary for attentiveness. A sense of optimism that one's efforts will result in rewarding outcomes, whether academically, socially, or within the family, is mandatory for a youngster to effectively engage in a task. Most children begin school with these feelings unless they have experienced significant emotional or social trauma. However, a lack of success (real or perceived) all too often dramatically affects a child's willingness to make the effort to comply or attempt to be successful. Abuse and neglect, depression, anxiety, and other emotional disturbances also have a major impact on a youngster's ability to attend and regulate behaviors.

Figure 2 is a graphic model of the balance between the characteristics required to maintain attention or protect one's attention zone. An effective, intact **distraction barrier** is necessary for an individual to maintain his or her attention zone and avoid the intrusion of various distractions. These distractions include internal (I) distractions, such as one's own thoughts, as well as external (E) distractions, including sound, movement, and environmental stimulation. The integrity or resistance of the distraction barrier requires adequate neurotransmitters, motivation and effort, stamina, and emotional comfort. When the distraction barrier is intact, the individual is able to reflect away the possible intrusive effects of these distractions. The individual can identify the distraction, decide not to respond to it, and actively inhibit his or her response instantaneously.

Figure 3 portrays the situation in early ADHD. Because of a lack of adequate neurotransmitters, information is processed too slowly, and an effective response to distractions is not possible. Labelling the distraction, deciding not to respond and attempting to ignore the intrusion takes so long, that the attention zone is pentetrated and attention lost. Uneven attention occures in ADHD because extra effort may overcome slow processing. Figure 3 also highlights the therapeutic value of environmental or behavioral management which typically involves home management strategies, school accommodations, educational support services and psychological therapies. Despite the relative weakness of neurtransmitters, effective, timely implementation of these treatments can allow for maintenance of a relatively adequate distraction barrier. If motivation/effort, emotional comfort, and stamina can be preserved, the individual's attention zone is protected and therefore allows reasonable success.

Figure 4 defines the evolution of ADHD symptoms' effect on motivation and effort. A youngster will continue to make the effort toward success until he or she recognizes that this effort is not only unsuccessful but also produces chronic disappointment and discouragement. These self-perceptions are often accentuated by adults who do not understand the cause of the child's underachievement and the effects of the child's frustrations and disappointments. A youngster may maintain a conceptual desire for success, but under these circumstances his or her effort is likely to become erratic and uneven. Eventually, in order to protect themselves emotionally, they will no longer aspire to success and "give up" by avoiding challenging tasks. This usually unconscious decision provides emotional protection, since these youngsters do not anticipate a marginal effort to be successful. A poor outcome no longer leads to the same feelings of disappointment. While adults view this transition as being disastrous and counterproductive, holding back on one's efforts for the child represents an emotional coping strategy. As motivation and effort disappear, the stamina or physical energy

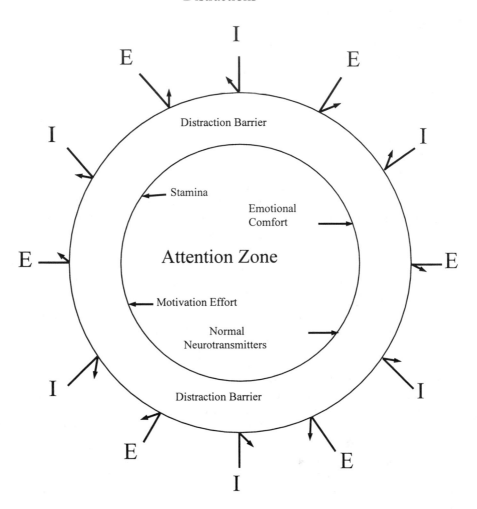

Figure 2
Balance Between Characteristics

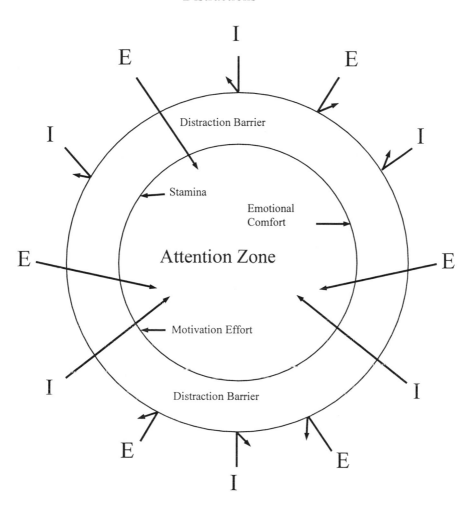

Figure 3
Early ADHD

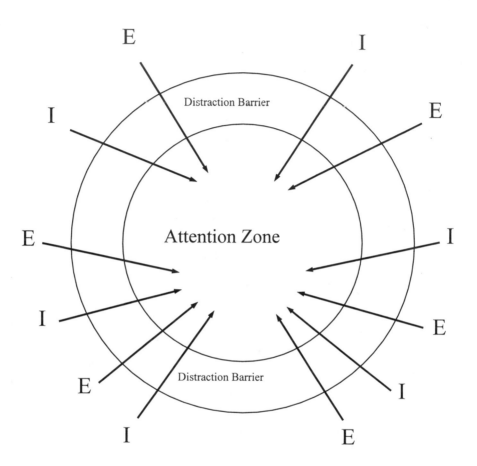

Figure 4
Evolution of ADHD Symptoms

invested in any effort becomes limited. Sleep and eating symptoms may develop. Also, youngsters with chronic medical conditions may have stress-related flare-ups requiring treatment.

The youngster's reduced motivation and effort lead to adult discipline responses, which typically have further emotional consequences for the child or adolescent. Depression and anxiety disorders may occur, leading to a downward spiraling in function and resulting in acting-out, antisocial, or self-destructive behavior. Unfortunately, the connection between the youngster's original developmental problem (ADHD) and these physical and emotional consequences is frequently not recognized. Adults often further aggravate the problem through more intense controlling or punishing responses. This scenario leads to a total destruction or collapse of the distraction barrier, leaving the individual unable to maintain his or her attention zone. Effective treatment, through sustaining motivation and effort, stamina, and emotional comfort, in addition to supporting neurotransmitter inadequacies with medication, can allow individuals with ADHD to maintain their distraction barrier and preserve their attention zone. Obviously, an earlier recognition of ADHD and treatment can avoid the physical and emotional consequences that make the condition much more difficult to treat. Unfortunately, the emergence of emotional responses can begin at quite a young age. However, it is never too late. Restitution of this complicated medical, social, and psychological interaction is possible when the origin of an individual's difficulties is understood, the preceding scenario is intercepted, and effective intervention occurs.

Figures 2 through 4 may be particularly useful in helping children and adolescents understand the nature of their attention disorder. For school-aged children, terms such as *attention zone* and *distraction barrier* are compatible with their video game experience. This model can be simplified by highlighting stamina, effort, and neurotransmitter characteristics if the child has not experienced emotional consequences as a result of her or his difficulties.

Adolescents may benefit by a graphic display of what they have experienced through their childhood into their teenage years. Their sense of chaos may be reduced by the awareness that professionals understand (to some extent) the results of their original difficulty with attention.

Dr. Russell Barkley has proposed another similar model for understanding ADHD. He believes that the symptoms of ADHD relate to an inability to postpone responsiveness appropriate to a particular situation or social cue. Individuals with ADHD have the capacity to control, organize, and respond with appropriate behavior. Their biggest difficulty lies in delaying responses. Delayed responses require the skills of prolonging an event in one's mind, separating feelings from facts, allowing for time to internally talk to oneself, and breaking apart and recombining events and information. The last step requires taking information or incoming messages apart, analyzing them for content or meaning, and then recombining their parts into a new message or response. ADHD individuals are not able to delay responsiveness in order for all of these necessary processes to occur. All of the preceding stages require adequate time and processing efficiency in order to delay or inhibit responses and allow planned behavioral responses.

OTHER CAUSES OF ADHD SYMPTOMS

A number of other medical, social, and emotional factors can lead to ADHD symptoms. These include but are not limited to the following.

Medical Factors

- Prenatal exposure to alcohol, cocaine, and lead, among many other toxic agents or drugs
- Prenatal factors that affect the nutrition of the developing fetus and lead to a baby being born small for his or her gestational age
- Neglect early in life while the nervous system is in a critical stage of development
- Uncommon metabolic disturbances that affect nervous system development and functioning
- Mental retardation
- Pervasive developmental delays
- Autism
- Several chromosomal or genetic syndromes (e.g., Down's syndrome)
- Medication prescribed for chronic medical conditions (e.g., asthma)
- Chronic sleep disorders and fatigue
- Difficult temperament

Emotional Factors

- Emotional, physical, or sexual abuse leading to chronic anxiety, depression, or distrust
- Anxiety disorders
- Depression

- Feeling of unacceptability resulting from continual criticism and negative reaction from adults, especially important caretakers

Behavioral Factors

- Inappropriate efforts to help a child learn
- Lack of academic and social success
- Mislearned behavioral profile based on adult responses to early behavioral patterns

REFERENCES

Barkley, R. (1993). The ADHD report: Vol. 1, No. 5. A new theory of ADHD. New York: Guilford Press.
Barkley, R. (1994). The ADHD report: Vol. 2, No. 2. More on the new theory of ADHD. New York: Guilford Press.

5

Adults with ADHD

Many individuals continue to have symptoms of ADHD that affect their functioning as adults. The incidence of ADHD among adults is not fully known. It is known, however, that approximately 80% of ADHD children will continue to have symptoms into their adolescence. The number of adolescents who continue to have symptoms into adulthood is not fully known because of the recent increase in the number of adults being diagnosed with ADHD. One study has estimated that the rate of ADHD declines by about 50% every 5 years. Based on this formula, it is anticipated that approximately 0.8% of 20-year-olds and 0.05% of 40-year-olds will appropriately be diagnosed with ADHD.

CHARACTERISTICS OF ADULT ADHD

Many adults with ADHD experience success in various areas of their lives. However, the requirements and the energy demands necessary to achieve that success, whether it be social, vocational, academic, or recreational, are often greater because of their ADHD symptoms. Some of the symptoms are a continuation of their childhood and adolescent experiences, while others are more specific to the demands of adult life. Many adults with ADHD have sought counseling on numerous occasions because of their continued sense of frustration, discouragement, and difficulty with interpersonal relationships. Often, they have a sense of discomfort about the relative lack of control they seem to have over their lives. Various characteristics have been described as being typical, and a number of formal criteria for adult ADHD have been suggested. A list of common symptoms follows.

1. A general sense of underachievement

2. Chronic procrastination

3. Organizational difficulties

4. Lack of completion of projects or a chronic lack of accomplishment of goals

5. Attempts to complete multiple projects simultaneously without adequate follow-through

6. Verbal impulsiveness

7. A continuous search for a high level of stimulation in experiences

8. An intolerance of boredom

9. Difficulty following proper or expected procedures in communicating with coworkers and superiors

10. Distractibility in combination with daydreaming or tuning out involuntarily

11. Impatience and a low frustration tolerance

12. Impulsive decision making

13. Restlessness

14. Excessive, incessant worrying

15. Mood swings

16. A general sense of chronic insecurity

17. A tendency toward addictive behaviors

18. Inaccurate self-perceptions regarding skills and abilities

19. Chronic difficulty with self-esteem

20. General inefficiency in terms of completion of daily tasks

21. Inability to follow through with tasks

If an adult is to meet the criteria for ADHD, these symptoms need to have been present during childhood, whether or not a formal evaluation occurred or a diagnosis was made. A review of historical records documenting functional difficulty in childhood is typically necessary. Corroborating the individual's self-observations by obtaining information from parents, spouses, and significant others is desirable to confirm the presence of these perceived symptoms and their impact on the adult's life. A medical assessment and psychiatric evaluation are important to rule out significant medical or emotional problems as the cause of the individual's symptoms. As in childhood, the diagnosis of ADHD is inherently subjective and clinical. There is no specific diagnostic test. However, also as in childhood, it is desirable to gather as much information as possible before proceeding with treatment. An individual approach to the adult's needs must be based on a complete assessment of those needs and the development of a personalized intervention program.

INTERVENTIONS

Intervention programs for adults require the same considerations as those for children and adolescents. Psychological therapies are usually required. Individual therapy can allow diagnosed adults better insight as to the impact of ADHD symptoms on their lives and the personal emotional consequences of those symptoms. Strategies can be developed that allow for improved task completion, work production, interpersonal relationships, and mood management. Coaching is often helpful to improve time management, priority setting, financial management, organizational skills, and job performance. For individuals who are having difficulty sustaining meaningful employment, a vocational assessment defining their strengths and weaknesses and job goals can help to enhance self-sufficiency and job stabilization.

Medical interventions can be extremely helpful to adults with ADHD. Stimulant medications identical to those used in childhood cases can often enhance performance, improve social interactional skills, and improve overall mood. Antidepressants and other psychoactive medications are frequently required either in conjunction with stimulant medications or as an independent treatment.

An individual is never too old to seek evaluation and treatment. Effectively treated adults with ADHD are extremely gratified by the efforts made to improve their life, regardless of their age. They often feel that the world of opportunity has dramatically expanded for them. According to one young man in his late 20s, "My life began yesterday," after his first day of medication.

Many adults identify themselves during the evaluation and treatment of their child. They also recognize that dealing with their own attention disorder symptoms often results in greater success in managing their child's needs. Many spouses and significant others are gloriously happy when their mate is effectively treated and opportunities for effective, meaningful communication have been dramatically enhanced.

A major challenge for adults with ADHD involves the education and understanding of employers and coworkers about ADHD in general and about their needs in particular. Just as effective treatment of ADHD in childhood and adolescence has proven that this population can be extremely successful academically and socially, so will the experience among adults prove the desirability of an employee whose ADHD is effectively managed.

6

The Impact of ADHD
on Families

The presence of an ADHD child, adolescent, or adult within a family typically affects all family members in multiple ways:

"He's driving us crazy."

"If only he weren't such a problem, we'd have a great family."

"He's such a pain. I can't even have friends over."

"He's such a nice boy. If he could only control his behavior better."

"Since we've learned how to help our child with ADHD, it seems like we're better parents to all of the children."

"Don't bring that boy over to my house. He ruins all my special antiques."

"If he'd only leave the dog alone, he could come over to play."

"Don't you know what a bad influence your son is on my daughter? I can't allow him to play here anymore."

"Now that Tommy has been treated, we can see what a talented and creative kid he was all along."

"Boy, we never knew he was so bright. He's so proud of himself."

    "All my husband and I do is argue about managing his behavior."

"When you write the prescription for his Ritalin, please write one for Valium for me."

"Will our family ever get along?"

"What do you mean he can't help himself?"

"What do I tell the rest of the kids?"

"The teachers can't believe the difference. We're so proud of him."

"I can't make special rules for him. What will the rest of the kids say?"

These comments describe the impact of an ADHD child or adolescent within an immediate and extended family. Depending on the severity of symptoms, all families will experience an alteration in their communication patterns and dynamics if there are one or several ADHD family members. The individual's impact on family functioning varies tremendously depending on his or her specific symptoms and the severity of the symptoms, as well as a variety of family characteristics. Many families are understanding, while others are devastated and, on occasion, destroyed by the individual's symptoms. Some of the family characteristics that determine the impact of an ADHD child or adolescent are:

1. The strength of the parents' relationship with each other

2. The preexisting level of family functioning

3. The communication level within the family

4. The family's emotional, economic, and time resources

5. Age, gender, and skills of the individual's siblings

6. The presence of other family members with special needs or chronic illnesses

7. Other sources of family stress, including financial or job stress and stress resulting from the needs of extended family members

This chapter presents various scenarios regarding effects on parents, parental communication with the ADHD child, and sibling relationships. It is important to note that the presence of an ADHD individual in a family may not always have a significant negative impact. In many families, there is true parental collaboration, mutual emotional support between parents, adequate individual attention to siblings, and a generally optimistic perspective, which can create a full maintenance of family integrity and emotional comfort for all members. In order for this to be accomplished, the potential impact on all family members must be addressed as part of the initial evaluation process and as a management plan is developed. Often families begin to gain a better understanding of their communication patterns as they learn to help the ADHD individual, thus enhancing the harmony within the family. Many parents find that they better support the needs of all of their children once they individualize their parenting approach by virtue of skills learned with their ADHD child or adolescent. The management of family needs can be just as successful as the management of the individual ADHD child's or adolescent's needs.

PARENTAL RELATIONSHIP

The presence of an ADHD individual can stress even the most secure relationships between parents. Prior to an evaluation, parents often blame each other for the child's behavioral difficulties. One particular event or situation that should have been handled differently is often presumed to be the cause of the problem. A prenatal event (for example, inadequate compliance with prenatal care directions or dangerous behavior during pregnancy) may allow the father to blame the mother for causing the youngster's problems:

"If you had only taken your vitamins every day, he'd be okay."
"You never should have taken that motorcycle ride in the third trimester."

Emotional stress caused by marital discord or relationship problems during pregnancy is often believed to lead to a child who will have behavioral difficulties:

"You were yelling at me through the whole pregnancy. How could a baby develop right?"
"I needed your attention while I was pregnant and you were never there."
"If you were only home when I started my labor and I got to the hospital sooner, he'd be fine."

Parents need to discuss openly the feelings created by these presumed causes of a youngster's behavioral and learning difficulties to alleviate any ongoing resentment and guilt and move on to a phase of collaboration in treating the youngster with ADHD.

Many different perinatal events have been presumed to be the cause of child behavioral difficulties. In fact, however, very few of these occurrences have been proven to be the cause, and very few have been proven to heighten the risk for a child of having behavioral difficulties. Again, a parent may hold his or her partner responsible for causing some of these birth-related events and being the cause of the child's difficulty. These presumptions need to be discussed during the evaluation of the child to clear the air and allow for further collaboration.

Parenting styles often differ within a successful relationship. When the children are doing well, these differences are generally accepted and tolerated. However, when one or several children are functioning poorly, parents will often attribute their difficulties to their partner's parenting style. Unfortunately, this perception often worsens the situation, even though the differences may have been unrelated to the cause of a youngster's problems.

Parents who perceive their partner's style as being inappropriate or causing problems often polarize each other to extremes. For example, the liberal parent becomes more liberal to compensate for the presumed negative effects of the harsh parent's approach. The harsh parent, seeing the liberal parent becoming more lax, intensifies his or her harshness to balance the relaxed approach. Ultimately, both parents wind up far more extreme in their approach than they ever intended. These extremes generally are not helpful to an ADHD child or adolescent, who requires structure, defined expectations and consistency in terms of management. The youngster becomes confused because of the mixed messages he or she receives and may give up trying to satisfy anybody's needs. He or she may also learn to manipulate a situation by playing one parent against the other.

Since the ADHD child or adolescent often monopolizes a significant amount of family time, the relationship between parents can become overly dependent upon the parenting successes or failures in regard to that child. A lack of regular success, along with squabbling over parenting style differences, may overwhelm the preexisting strength of the relationship. Many emotionally supportive relationships can tolerate this stress. Other weaker, less firm relationships can be destroyed, however, with the parents no longer desiring to support each other or becoming antagonistic. Separation and divorce may, unfortunately, result. Some families in which the basic marital relationship is weak will overfocus on the child as the cause of their problems or on the need for them to stay together in a bad relationship on the child's behalf.

It is important to recall that if a youngster has ADHD, there is a 15% to 25% chance that a parent (or both of the parents) will have ADHD. This circumstance certainly complicates family life and may enhance the stress in a marital relationship. Some parents with an ADHD partner will say, "It feels like I have two ADHD kids." An ADHD parent may be disorganized and inefficient, requiring more time and energy in terms of vocational and daily endeavors. In addition, some ADHD adults will continue to be impulsive and to have poor social interactional skills, causing them difficulty in effectively communicating with their partner and guiding and directing the child in a consistent, effective manner. Successfully living with an ADHD adult may require a great deal of patience, understanding, and time on the part of the non-ADHD parent, leaving fewer resources for the ADHD child.

STRESS ON FAMILY RESOURCES

The presence of an ADHD child or adolescent often drains the resources of parents. Three areas of stress are emotions, finances, and time.

Emotional Resources

Emotional resources are drained because of continuing confusion about the appropriate way to manage the child and the necessity to constantly react to criticism of the child by school personnel, grandparents, uncles and aunts, neighbors, team coaches, friends, parents of peers, and so forth. Unfortunately, the explanation that "My child has ADHD and we're doing our best to help him" rarely satisfies critics and often leaves the parents feeling inadequate and guilty. In situations in which divorce occurs, the youngster's accentuated needs often exaggerate the situation because the parents continue to be polarized, disagreeing about the explanation for the youngster's problem and struggling over decisions regarding interventions.

Economic Resources

Drainage of economic resources is a realistic problem when a family attempts to understand and treat an ADHD youngster. The diagnostic process can be complicated, depending on the profile of the youngster's needs. Intervention, whether psychological, educational, or medical in nature, is a regular, often major expense that drains dollars that could have been used for the needs of the other children in the family or for general living or recreational purposes. There can be resentment over such expenditures, especially if the various interventions do not produce beneficial results.

Time

In today's hectic pace of life, time resources are limited and valuable for most busy parents. The presence of an ADHD child or adolescent often consumes a great deal of this precious time. Unfortunately, the other youngsters in the family who do not need or demand extra attention get less of their parents' available time. Love may be equally distributed among all of the children, but access to parents' time is important as well. If a child feels that he or she is being denied that time, he or she may become resentful or angry, and the parent will experience feelings of guilt.

SIBLING RELATIONSHIPS

Siblings are generally markedly affected by their ADHD brother or sister. In most families, siblings, especially those of younger ages, are expected to spend a great deal of time together and to interact playfully and peacefully, often for extended periods of time. The ADHD youngster's behavioral characteristics often do not allow for such a scenario. Depending on the youngster's behavioral difficulty, he or she will often be overbearing, bossy, intrusive, inadvertently disrespectful of other siblings' space, and unwilling to share. Furthermore, the child may have an impulsive need for immediate gratification and may be extremely sensitive to the attention received by siblings. All of these characteristics lead to a breakdown in the desire for peaceful, enjoyable, and gratifying play. Complaints about the ADHD youngster to parents cause great strife. The parent is aware that taking sides is not helpful but realizes that the ADHD youngster may well be the primary cause of the interactional problems. This results in mixed messages being sent to both the ADHD child and her or his siblings.

Siblings often grow angry and resentful of the ADHD youngster. They attempt to avoid playing with their sibling or respond with the same behavior as the sibling, leading to more negative interactions and parental complaints. These problems can often escalate as the children get older.

Once the diagnosis of ADHD is made, the parents have a dilemma. Do they inform the siblings of their brother's or sister's diagnosis and ask them to be more understanding or even to become a therapist for their sibling, or do they simply work on improving the ADHD youngster's behavior profile and hope that beneficial results are forthcoming? There is no simple solution. Informing siblings of a youngster's ADHD diagnosis may make the ADHD child even more vulnerable to the feelings of siblings, who now have a specific label to use in harassing that child. Asking a sibling to become a therapist by understanding and accepting a brother's or sister's behavioral disorder sometimes enhances the existing resentment. Some siblings have been known to "spread the word" to neighborhood and school friends about their sibling's diagnosis in order to play out their unresolved anger. The most appropriate strategy to use with siblings will depend on their age, specifics characteristics of their relationship with the ADHD child, and other family factors.

As mentioned, an ADHD child expends an enormous amount of resources within a family. The excessive expenditure of emotions, dollars, and time often limits the availability of those resources for the child's siblings. Children will often hold their parents, rather than the ADHD child, accountable for this problem. Also, their resentment may result in the development of behavioral and school-related problems because they desire the same attention received by the ADHD brother or sister. At an early age, youngsters may mimic their siblings' behavior in order to gain a parental response.

SPECIAL FAMILY SITUATIONS

Divorce, blended family, and single-parent situations often add a complicating dimension to the management of an ADHD child or adolescent. Unfortunately, divorced parents often are further polarized regarding the appropriate management of their child than they were during their marriage. Parents' criticisms of each other's parenting approach often undermine the effectiveness of both and leave the child confused as to how to satisfy the parents' needs. Children often feel that they are in the middle, being pushed and pulled in each direction and having to choose between parents, which is an impossible dilemma. Because divorced parents often disagree about parenting, it is common for one parent to support the ADHD diagnosis while the other blames poor parenting ("I don't have any problems at my house. He'd be okay if she were a better parent."). Such disagreements often postpone or preclude effective intervention. For example, the youngster is often sent mixed messages about the appropriateness and safety of medication, leaving the youngster confused and often resistant to taking and benefitting from any medication. Different behavioral expectations in different parental environments represent an additional source of confusion.

While consistent parenting is necessary in any divorce situation, it is especially important for ADHD youngsters, who require structure, defined expectations, consistency, and regular positive reinforcement if their behavior is to be appropriately regulated. Collaborative parenting in divorce situations can and does occur, and it can well serve the needs of an ADHD youngster. As with any children in a divorce situation, the key to emotional health for the children relates to parents being as amicable as possible and providing messages of continued support and availability. Each parent must avoid undermining the parenting skills, love, and concern of the other. Divorced children can never feel as though they are caught in a struggle between their parents, nor can they be told by one parent that the other is incapable of meeting their needs. The needs of the child must be a major concern for both parents.

Single parents often have difficulty in finding enough time and energy to provide direction, guidance, and full attention to their children's special needs. They have little time and energy left after providing financial security for their family and still meeting their own personal needs. These roles may be overwhelming and may not allow a parent to be a therapist and an effective interventionist for an ADHD youngster. Such limitations have little to do with parental motivation and effort, but available resources may be stressed nonetheless. It becomes increasingly important for the single parent to use available community and school resources as well as parent support systems. As highlighted throughout this chapter, success with an ADHD child or adolescent is certainly attainable for a single parent with reasonable effort and use of the resources of the community and, if available, those of extended family members and friends.

7

What the Kids Have to Say

M ost youngsters have significant insight into their own ADHD symptoms and the impact of those symptoms on their lives. Many children and adolescents also recognize the impact of their symptoms on others, even though they often appear oblivious. Evaluation of such children typically involves formally or informally surveying adults regarding their perceptions and opinions, with the youngster often being observed and tested. Unfortunately, frequently youngsters are not asked how they perceive their problems, what personal efforts they feel they have made to remedy the situation, or what adults could do to provide the most help.

A carefully planned interview, conducted in a quiet, nondistracting situation at the developmental level of the child, can provide enormously valuable information. Some level of trust must first be established between the interviewing professional and the child. It is also important that professionals describe themselves as caring a great deal about kids, as being experts on children's problems, as having been able to help many other children with similar problems, and as being advocates for kids, not just parents. The interview cannot be rushed. There needs to be enough time for youngsters to express themselves at a comfortable pace and for the interviewer to fill in gaps with "small talk."

KIDS' MESSAGES

Youngsters of various ages were asked to talk about their ADHD in a spontaneous way or to answer the three following questions:

1. What has it been like for you to have ADHD?

2. How have the treatments helped you, and which treatments have helped the most?

3. What would you tell the parents of a child with ADHD that would help them better understand and know what to do to help their child?

Young Adults

The following is a poem written by a 23-year-old who had symptoms of ADHD throughout his childhood and adolescence and into adulthood. He is a talented musician and has begun writing poetry as a vehicle for personal expression. The poem, titled "Birth of a Man," represents his reflections as an individual with ADHD.

Looking back
   On the sands of time
I am the man
   Of my boyhood eyes.

A boy with desire,
   Struggling through life,
Now a grown man,
   But not without strife.

Seeing the days
   As I began to grow,
Those were the ways
   That led me to know.

A man with intelligence
   Mind never at ease,
Plagued through life
   With a mental disease.

Not able to concentrate
   For only a few
Lived a life
   Much harder than you.

Hard as it seemed,
   Fighting through school
Referred to often
   As only a fool.

Artistic ability
   Poured out like a vase.
Music was it,
   His serenity place.

A gifted musician
   Notes from the bell,
That mighty trumpet
   Broke his thick shell.

Given great confidence,
   Feeling renewed,
Playing beautiful music
   Is all he would do.

Only a few
   Were better than he.
A God-given gift
   that all could see.

Watching that boy
   Change through time,
I am the man
   Poured out of my boyhood eyes.

Like windows in a house
   What he saw, I could see.
That tortured young boy
   Turned out to be me.

A man with integrity
   And courage to see
All that I needed
   Was to accept me for me.

A blind man can't see,
   Without his glass
Medicine for me,
   Connected my past.

The wild young boy
   Untamed and crazed
Who knew it was me,
   Before years of age?

A grown up man
   With a tortured mind,

That was the boy
    That I left behind.

Looking back
    Over the years;
Seeing the boy
    With so many fears.

Now seeing my life
    With the light that died,
I am the grown man
    From within my boyhood eyes.—Lyons Whitmore

Another young adult (described by his parents as having been impulsive throughout his life) who was academically successful until college portrayed his lifelong symptoms as follows:

> When I first realized that I probably had a problem, it was maybe in high school when I would just sort of do things, not really having a reason, or say things that I'd pretty much regret right after I'd say them. You know, you'd just say kinda just something, the first thought that would pop into your head and it would be the first thing that came out of your mouth. It was an awful, awful feeling. Sometimes you'd just sort of hurt other people and it wasn't right. . . . I just kinda let it go with my personality. People would call me a "smart ass" or something like that, and I guess more or less it was true. But it was just something I couldn't control. I mean, I probably could have had I sat and thought about it, but overall it was just a tough thing.

He describes his distractibility:

> I was wondering a lot about the way that my mind worked. And I saw myself in class, and I would be looking up at the teacher and I would, this was the one I remember the most, I would look up at the fan and I would see the fan and think to myself, "Wow, I wonder how many times that fan is going around?" And then something else would just grab my attention, and before you know it 15 or 20 minutes had gone by and I'd have to sit down and scribble everything the teacher has written down on the board. It was annoying and amazing.

Adolescents and Younger Children

Several younger youth described what it's been like for them to have ADHD.

I am distracted easily and have trouble doing work in a noisy area.

It's very annoying when you try to listen and someone moves and you just focus on them.

I used to have a hard time staying in my seat in school. My grades weren't good because I was off in a daze a lot during class. I always forgot to do my work and sometimes I wouldn't turn it in at all. I just wanted to play soccer.

[School] work is really easy, but I don't concentrate hard enough to make it simple for me.

It's hard for me to do my work and it's too noisy and I tell the teacher. . . . I go off in front of the class and I tell the teacher and she calms it down. I don't like it that much. It's hard for me to do my work. But I get it done. I do like school and everybody likes it, but when they . . . it's like Halloween or something and they go . . . they talk too much and they yell and scream, I don't like it.

When I try and pay attention, all my energy is focused on paying attention, so I don't get what's going on. And when I try and, like, understand what's going on, then I don't pay any attention, so I can't do my work. A lot of the time I need space, like, just to clear my mind and stuff. But sometimes when I get the space, then I abuse, like, my privileges and that's what gets me in trouble.

What I think about having ADHD is it's kind of interesting because sometimes you don't think about that you're all wound up or something and you are, and you might make a fool out of yourself or something.

It has been hard for me and now that I have been on the medicine, it has been easier for me. I started taking the medicine when I was 9 years old. I am now 15. Now I look back to before I started taking the medicine and look back when I started taking, and what a difference. When I was 9, I told my mom, "You know how you are always asking me how are you feeling? Well I feel better now. I'm not moving inside, and I feel more calm."

Having ADHD is kind of like an insecurity. It is like being insecure and not being able to control what you do. When you do something you just do it and then you realize what you've done. That's kind of what it's like.

To give some examples of that, like, for instance my sister and me. Sometimes we don't get along. I'll sit there and we kind of argue. She kind of makes me mad, and then I feel like, you know, I feel like hitting. I feel like reacting. And what I'll do, I mean, I'll just, you know, all of a sudden my mind will kind of go blank a little bit, you know, and then I'll, you know, the first thing that comes up is hit her if she's making me mad. But it's not like something's telling me to do it. I just do it, and then I realize what I've done and realize how it was really stupid. Why would you do that? That's what it's like. It's really kind of confusing to talk about.

It affects my life, like I get bored very easily if I'm not doing something and get wild if I'm bored.

Sometimes in class I'll feel hyper or energetic and I'll want to, you know, get up and move around but I can't because I'm in class. It's really weird, you know. It's like a cat, kind of. You can't hold him, you know, like hold him down. He's going to want to get up. He's going to want to run away.

It's hard having ADHD because you have to work at it all the time. You have to work at calming down, calming yourself and keeping yourself from fidgeting around. If you don't, then it makes it a lot harder for you at home and at school. At school, kids with ADHD need to know how to calm themselves, how to keep cool, and how to sit there and listen to the teacher. And when to move around and when to speak. Because if you just talk all the time, then you're probably going to get in trouble or not learn as much if you're off task.

Most everything is like any other kid's life but you have a hard time controlling anger, disappointment, and temper.

The biggest problem is not being able to pay attention to things I found boring.

More Thoughts

When asked why his parents brought him for an evaluation, one 6-year-old answered, "The teacher wanted me to come in because I don't do my work fast enough. I don't have enough time to finish because there is too much noise. Kids make fun of me because I'm slow and then they get my attention. Then I have even more trouble doing my work."

Some youngsters will identify aggravating factors that worsen their ability to regulate their behavior. One 8-year-old, when asked why his parents brought him for an evaluation, said, "The teacher thinks I can't sit still. It's hard for me. My mom gives me vitamins every morning and I do better when I don't take them [because of the sugar contained in the vitamins] and when my mom puts brown sugar on my cereal, I have a real problem."

Treatment Observations

Most youngsters are quite aware of how treatments benefit them. However, they tend to attribute too much of their success to the medication, even though their role has been emphasized throughout the treatment process.

One youngster addressed his comments to those who are skeptical about the need for and benefits of medication:

And what I'd have to say to those people who are skeptical, you didn't really ask for this but I'm going to give it anyway, umm . . . they're ignorant. They just don't know any different. Maybe they're afraid of what it is. I would just have to say that they're ignorant, like a lot of people, maybe even me. I could understand them being that way, though. But they just need to take one good look at those people who it really has helped and those people that are successful from it. And maybe somewhere along the line they can understand and realize that there is such a thing. I think that's all I can really say at this time.

A middle school youngster reflected on his experience in a social skills group:

I can't remember what grade I was in, but I would always go on Wednesdays. I remember on Wednesday nights there was like a group for kids with ADHD. There was a group, like parents and kids. Kids were taken off to one place to another separate room where they had all this stuff and everything for them to use, and they were put there and they got to do stuff. Because kids get to meet other kids about their age, maybe some older or some younger that have ADHD. They help because they get to see other kids—they know that they're not alone. There are other kids out there that do have this, and the parents get to talk to other parents with kids and find out what they're doing and the other parents get to find out what you're doing. So it helps both ways. It helped me meet kids who had it and they told me how they worked with it, and I told them how I did. And we learned something from each other. And that's the way it goes.

Another youngster spoke to his role in enhancing the effectiveness of his medication:

The reason why I think the Ritalin is helping me is because I work with it. And the other reason is just because I think it helps me a lot. I don't really know why it helps me, but it just helps me out a little and helps me a little longer too. The reason why it helps me is because I work with it and it helps me out too. And I don't get in trouble that much anymore. It helps a lot and my family helps by telling me when to take my medicine. My teacher helps me with when to take my medicine at school. And I feel I have attention disorder pretty bad, but I take medicine so I think I'll be alright in the future.

Still another youngster appreciated the improvements shown in regard to his impulsivity:

You know, and um, boy the medicine—the medicine, what it does is it helps to tell you, to bring you back and show you what you're going to do before you do it. The blankness that fills it. It fills you with thoughts about what you're going to do and why you shouldn't do it, and then it helps you not to do it. It has helped me a lot to control myself, you know, reaching out and grabbing something or hitting my sister or telling my mom cuss words, you know, cussing at people and getting me in trouble, and just all stupid stuff if you just stop and think, and that's what the medicine helps you to do.

One youngster recognized the value of medication in conjunction with his own personal strategies and his mom's coaching:

The medication helps me with calming myself down, ignoring people, ignoring the bratty Jeremy and Christian, and helps me with . . . my mom helps me with them too. Like, sometimes they take my chair away when I get up and then come back they're already in it. And sometimes I have an argument. But today I tried, umm, well today is November 12, 1996. I used a technique she told me. I went up, got up to sharpen my pencil. The kid named Christian got up and I didn't see him. He got in my chair. I came back and almost said, "Can I have my chair back?" And I knew he was going to say, "No, you got up." And I said, "Okay, I don't want that chair. I'd rather take another one. Besides that chair was broken anyway." And then I go and sit down. And then he thinks it isn't very fun and he goes off and sits somewhere else because if I want to sit there and I get up, my mom says that he knows he can get me in trouble by having an argument. The medication also helps me to get along on the playground. I think it makes me feel better about helping other people.

Another youngster spoke to the social aspect of ADHD and medication:

I found out from testing I had ADD. I thought it was a disease at first. My doctor told me that medicine would help. I tried Ritalin; it didn't work well . . . then Dexedrine and it helped a lot. When I took pills at school I found out other kids had it in my class. Will, Lindsey, and Jonathan. I felt a lot better because I wasn't the only child that had ADD.

This youngster had a gripe: "counsoling [counseling] helps, so does Cylert, but I wish they didn't have to use Latin for the name." Another complaint: "For the medication, the medicine should be some kind of another color because we have a light floor and we, sometimes on the bed when I wake up, my mom brings the medicine and we accidentally drop it on the bed, and since we have a dog who eats anything, I'm afraid he might find it and eat it and he might die. So it should be a little bit of a different color than white." Yet another: "The medicine is good and not good because sometimes when I put it in my mouth, my mouth is watery and I put it in my mouth and there is one certain kind that disintegrates and when it disintegrates it tastes awful. And so I think they should try to get one with the same stuff in it but one that had a kind of layer around it so it won't disintegrate, like a really hard layer. And, I'm done, and thank you for listening."

Youngsters' Advice

Many youngsters with ADHD have advice for everybody. The comments to follow were in response to the question "What would you tell parents of a child with ADHD that would help them better understand and know what to do to help their child?"

You should find a good doctor to help your child. Because I know how hard it is to have ADHD. I'm very thankful for the medicine I take every day. It has helped me out a lot, and it can help your child a lot too. It's not just finding a doctor for your child and taking him/her to see the doctor. It also takes a lot of love, patience, and working with your son/daughter.

The parents, since we have it, when they call the kid's name they should call their name once, wait a few minutes, then call them again and wait a few minutes again, and the third time they call them they wait one minute and call and tap them on the shoulder.

If a kid has ADHD or ADD and they have brothers and sisters, then the parents should not try to mask the problem away from the brothers and sisters. They should explain why the kid has to take medicine and try to have the siblings understand that there is kind of a problem or that have a special thing about the person with ADD or ADHD that they have different or need special help maybe, so then the brothers and sisters don't think that their ADHD sibling isn't, like, weird or has a really bad problem they can't solve. The parents should explain to younger brothers and sisters or older brothers and sisters what the problem is and how they're helping the kid with ADHD or ADD and why they might clap their hands or why this happens or why that happens, and I think that's all pretty much about all I want.

The parents should know that taking the medication morning, day, and night is hard and they should know not to lose their temper with us kids and they should try to walk a mile in our shoes.

Also, you need to encourage your child to do sports, like, do after-school activities and stuff. If he's rambunctious after he gets home from school, ask him to see if he would like to do a sport or something. Have him put, like, lift weights or put that energy to something good . . . constructive. If that works, then that's good because they are learning to channel and you're helping them channel their energy from ADHD into something useful, which would be sports.

Also, like, for kids and parents—see if you can get them in volunteer work—something constructive. Like check with the U.S. West—they got Christmas in April and with the Pioneer Paint Company. They are painting schools. They're, like, going to junior highs and elementary schools and painting maps of the U.S. for the kids. I'm in it. I've been working on that. I'm doing volunteer work.

Another thing is that parents shouldn't put kids who are a little bit, what is that word? If they think their kid is a little bit hyperactive, you know, then they shouldn't put kids on hyperactive medicine thinking that the kid is hyperactive and have the kid kind of "jolt" up even more hyperactive, so they kind of like stimulate him, you know. So, if it doesn't calm him down it makes him more hyperactive, they should take him off right then.

A middle schooler had advice for other kids with ADHD:

And maybe for kids out there, help your parents out. They're trying everything for you. Don't do this just to spite them. Don't, like, even with the medicine, don't try to act like it just to spite them. No, they want to help you. And I know you might not like doing this—I didn't when I first started, but it's helping you. If you—do you want to be fidgeting and be yelled at all the time? If you do, that's your opinion, but me—I don't like it. I like to help out. . . .

And also, like I said before, it helps channel the energy. For kids, try your hardest to let the medicine work. That's what you gotta do. If you're still feeling different when you get home and you think you're going to be too rambunctious for the inside, go ride your bike or run or do something. If you have a punching bag, use it on that. Like take out your anger on the punching bag or the pillow or whatever you need. Just do it for something constructive. Don't, like, mess up the house or destroy stuff. No. Don't get caught up in stuff like that that will get you in trouble. That's not what you need to do. You need to put it to a good use. Like ADHD with all this energy. All this energy you need to put it to something . . . sports or working construction. So you can really do a lot of stuff with this energy. But you gotta remember—if you're working with stuff, be cool. Don't rush around because you can get hurt. And I know we don't want you to get hurt. Well, I hope this can help you guys because I know it has helped me.

Finally, one school-aged child, when he was told that the author was writing a book about ADHD for parents, suggested a title: "ADHD: A Parent Trap."

8

The Diagnosis of ADHD

The diagnosis of ADHD typically occurs on two levels. The first is quite simplistic: If a child appears unable to pay attention, or is hyperactive, distractible, or impulsive, he or she is presumed to have ADHD. This approach is not adequate because it does not allow for a full understanding of the cause of the youngster's difficulties or initiation of an effective treatment program. The second level addresses the many causal factors related to these symptoms and explores the presence of coexisting symptoms. The appropriate diagnostic process must be sufficiently thorough to ensure that all relevant factors determining a youngster's behavioral and functional profile are considered. A review of the youngster's health, development, temperamental profile (personality), and responses to life experiences, as well as a family history, is necessary since there is no single diagnostic test for ADHD.

BEHAVIORAL ASSESSMENT

Observational data from a variety of sources, including teachers, babysitters, caretakers, parents, and grandparents, are essential. Such information is often obtained through completion of questionnaires and surveys that allow for comparison of the child's scores with a national sample of children of the same age and gender. Accurate interpretation of these instruments requires that they be formally scored. Commonly used forms include the Conners Parents and Teachers Scales, the ADD-H Comprehensive Teacher

Rating Scale, the Attention Deficit Disorders Evaluation Scale, and the Achenbach Child Behavior Checklist Ages 4–18 (for both parents and teachers). Self-report scales for children and adolescents are available. These instruments are important because they provide insight into feelings and self-perceptions that the child may not be willing or able to verbalize. They also provide a statistical sample of children of the same age and gender for comparison purposes. The Achenbach Self Reporting Scale for Ages 11–18, like the parent and teacher forms, surveys emotional as well as attention deficit disorder symptoms. The Brown Attention Deficit Disorder Scale for Adolescents is appropriate for 12- to 18-year-olds and divides attentional difficulties into five components: activation, attention, effort, affect, and memory.

Interviews with the children or adolescents are important, regardless of age, to gain knowledge of their feelings about and understanding of:

- their problems

- their current level of functioning

- their strengths and weaknesses

- their emotional reactions to personal successes or inadequacies

- their relationship with the adults and peers in their life

- their desire for change or improvement

Such interviews also provide great insight into the children's personality and communication skills.

PHYSICAL ASSESSMENT

A current assessment of the youngster's overall health, nutrition, visual and auditory acuity, and physical, neurological, and neurodevelopmental status is important, both as a diagnostic measure and to rule out other causes of ADHD-type behavioral symptoms.

Traditionally available tests of neurological functioning such as EEGs, CT scans, and MRIs are not clinically useful unless there is strong consideration of a seizure disorder or other neurological diseases as a cause of the behavioral symptoms. There is also no currently available laboratory test to assess presumed biochemical or neurotransmitter variation in the nervous system.

A positive response to a drug trial with a psychostimulant such as Ritalin is not believed to be an appropriate independent diagnostic test for a variety of reasons. Children (especially young children) have the capacity for enhanced attentiveness with artificial maturation of their nervous system with medication on a brief basis, whether or not they have ADHD. In addition, the behavioral reaction of adults based on positive expectations with drug use may be more powerful in changing the youngster's behavior than the actual drug effect. When parents administer medication to their child, they and the child's teacher have the expectation of improvement. As a result, they may begin (for the first time) noticing positive behaviors they previously ignored because they were so focused on the negative aspects of the child's functioning. Naturally, the positive behavior is recognized and complimented, providing great encouragement to the child (perhaps for the first time). This reinforcement, rather than the medication, may be the reason for the improvement. Unfortunately, under these circumstances the medication is given credit for its apparent beneficial effects and the child is kept on medication unnecessarily. A drug trial as a diagnostic test also ignores the need to understand the youngster's coexisting symptoms so that the treatment program can be as comprehensive as necessary and produce the best possible long-term outcome.

COMPUTER TESTS

Computer-based tests of continuous performance have become popular in the assessment of impulsivity, inattention, and distractibility. The results of these tests must be correlated with all of the clinical data mentioned earlier to derive meaningful conclusions. These tests are not intended to be used as independent diagnostic tests; rather, they are merely a source of objective information. The Tests of Variables of Attention, the Conners Continuous Performance Test, and the Gordon Diagnostic System are the most commonly used programs.

The tasks involved in these tests are purposefully monotonous and boring. They challenge youngsters' ability to maintain their attention and arousal. Four major measurements are calculated:

1. Errors of omission that occur when the youngster should have responded but did not. These errors measure attention.

2. Errors of commission that occur when the youngster responded but should not have. These errors measure impulsivity.

3. Reaction time in milliseconds, which measures the speed at which the youngster responds.

4. Variability in reaction time over the total number of responses throughout the test. Individuals with ADHD tend to have a high level of inconsistency in terms of their response time.

These tests are generally administered in a quiet, nondistracting environment quite different from a busy classroom. These circumstances can sometimes make the results difficult to interpret. If youngsters have difficulty with the task, they may well have worse problems in school. If they do well, the diagnosis of ADHD can still be appropriate, depending on other information and on data derived from questionnaires and observations.

PSYCHOEDUCATIONAL ASSESSMENT

Psychoeducational testing can be useful in understanding the impact of attentional difficulties on academic functioning, in assessing the possibility of a coexisting learning or language difficulty, and in discovering the common profile for ADHD individuals on subscores of these tests. Tests of emotional functioning, often called projective tests, may be useful when these areas are considered to be important influences on the youngster's functioning.

THE TEAM APPROACH

The parents and the child are team members, along with the professional evaluator(s). A physician, particularly a pediatrician, should be actively involved in all evaluations. Pediatricians' background in neurology, child development, general health, and understanding of behavior and emotions qualifies them for this role. Various educational professionals are also necessary. At a minimum, completion of questionnaires by teachers is required. Educational diagnosticians and a school psychologist may be needed to conduct psychoeducational and intelligence tests, in addition to making classroom and test observations.

A psychologist may be required to explore emotional factors. Social workers or family counselors may be needed to investigate family issues that affect a child's or adolescent's functioning. A speech and language professional can conduct the appropriate test when speech or language processing disorders are considered. A physical or occupational therapist can assess coordination issues as needed. The "team" members may never actually get together in a single location, but they can effectively share information in writing and/or by phone. When necessary and possible, a true meeting may add a fuller dimension to the process. Any member of the team can serve as coordinator and collate all information.

The initial evaluator must determine, in collaboration with the parents, which if any of these professionals are required to conclude an adequate assessment. A decision also needs to be made as to whether education-related tests are taken through the public school or privately. Cost and convenience are benefits of using the school. Generally, tests can be administered privately in a more timely fashion because of the demands made on school psychologists and special educators.

It is unrealistic that most families will have the financial resources to employ a team of four or five professionals to evaluate their child. The initial evaluator must be aware of financial issues when making recommendations, and the following two questions should be answered:

How much will the additional evaluation add to the information necessary to create an appropriate intervention program?
Could the expenses incurred by these assessments better serve the needs of the ADHD child if they were used for treatment?

It is the responsibility of the initial evaluator to screen for other causal factor, coexisting disorder, and consequence data in order to answer these questions and make recommendations. Compromises and a practical approach based on available resources are often required without excessively sacrificing the quality of help for the youngster. Often it is possible to initiate treatment for one aspect of a child's needs while closely observing other features. For example, if self-esteem has suffered because of a lack of home and school success, the resilience of the child can be followed while enhancing success by means of environmental and medical interventions rather than assuming that counseling is immediately necessary.

As is true for most tasks or endeavors, the quality of the input will be reflected in the output or product. A thoughtful evaluation with a broad perspective is necessary for an individualized, optimally productive outcome for the ADHD child or adolescent. Self-education by parents prior to a diagnostic evaluation will allow selection of the most appropriate professional for initial contact. Parents should be prepared with relevant information (i.e., school testing results) and specific questions. If conclusions or recommendations are not fully understood, clarification should be sought until a comfort level is achieved. It is reasonable to question the relative value of further assessment and the goals of various interventions. Active parental involvement in the diagnostic process will enhance the value of the process for them and, especially, their child.

SUMMARY

An effective diagnostic process can be compared with the creation of a puzzle involving the preceding sources of information and data as the pieces. Since there is no single diagnostic test, this accumulation of information from various sources and perspectives is considered necessary. When the puzzle is completed, it may indicate a single diagnosis, reflect general coexisting diagnoses, or define a primary diagnosis with one or several consequences. More meaningful diagnostic data allows for the development of a more personalized, comprehensive treatment program.

9

General Treatment Principles

The intervention program for any ADHD child or adolescent must be individualized and carefully designed to meet the child's particular needs. As stressed throughout this book, youngsters with ADHD are much more different than they are alike. It makes sense, then, that a treatment program must not only meet the youngster's needs but take into account his or her strengths. All youngsters with ADHD have different

- Developmental profiles

- Temperaments or personalities

- Life experiences

- Family and cultural expectations

- Available resources

- School experiences and opportunities

- Levels of general health

- Stamina

- Chronic medical conditions and medications

- Personal aspirations, interests, and goals

- Skills

- Emotional responses to limitations caused by their ADHD symptoms

- Core ADHD symptom severities

- Coexisting symptoms

All of these factors must be considered when designing an intervention program. The program must also be compatible with the parents' personal needs, perceptions, and resources. Medication is frequently the only intervention used in helping a youngster with ADHD. While many studies have shown the short-term benefit of medication for core ADHD symptoms (hyperactivity, inattention, distractibility, and impulsivity), there is no evidence that long-term goals, such as enhanced academic performance or social adaptation, are achieved with this approach.

The primary treatment for ADHD involves environmental or behavioral management programs both at home and at school. This includes home management programs, educational accommodations, and psychological therapies. These approaches, alone or in combination with medical therapy, are called **multimodal** or combination therapies. Medication should be viewed as a facilitator or enhancer of these environmental efforts, allowing youngsters better behavioral regulation so that they can benefit and learn from these efforts on their behalf. For example, an improved ability to pay attention and focus can allow a youngster to learn more successfully in response to a special education program. Environmental and behavioral efforts are the essential elements of treatment programs for all children, adolescents, and young adults appropriately diagnosed with ADHD; medication remains optional. This statement should not be misinterpreted to mean that medication should be considered a last-ditch effort when all else has failed. If this were the approach, a youngster's self-esteem would be damaged significantly, and the likelihood of an overall successful outcome would be greatly reduced.

For most children or adolescents, reasonable environmental efforts on their behalf should be implemented at the earliest stage of treatment. Medical treatment can then be considered based on level of improvement and the specific profile of remaining symptoms. There is no exact formula to use in determining how long to continue with environmental approaches before considering medication. All of the factors listed earlier need to be considered when this decision is discussed. Some youngsters will, in fact, need medication at the initial stages of their treatment as a result of a crisis situation, an extreme inability to control themselves (making the success of environmental efforts highly improbable), or significant emotional concerns (eliminating the youngster's motivation for or interest in any intervention).

The need for ongoing environmental and behavioral management persists for an extended period of time regardless of the addition of medication.

The specific approaches used with children, adolescents, or young adults may vary tremendously because of the differences among individuals with ADHD. The treatment decision process is best accomplished through skilled professionals working closely together with the youngster and his or her family. Treatment programs should involve short- and long-term goals with regularly scheduled reviews of progress and necessary adaptation or changes in specific strategies. As in the evaluation and initial treatment design, the youngsters themselves should be important participants in the review and adaptation phase. They must always feel as though parents, teachers, and clinicians are listening carefully to them. They must also be aware that the adults may not always agree with them and may direct them to do things in their best interest.

The remainder of this book focuses on various treatment approaches that have been shown to be useful for youngsters with ADHD. Remember, all youngsters with ADHD are more different than they are alike. These approaches are discussed briefly in the sections to follow.

FAMILY SELF-EDUCATION

In the family self-education approach, often called demystification, all family members learn about the origins of ADHD and the full scope of symptoms. A fuller understanding of the behaviors and performance difficulties experienced by the youngster with ADHD is the goal. The "mystery" is removed from the situation. This education is intended to remove the chaos regarding a youngster's behavior and provide answers to the following questions:

Why does the youngster appear to be unable to control her or his behavior?
Why are there are such marked fluctuations in behavior over time?
What is behind the youngster's particular emotional response to his or her difficulties?

A resources chapter at the end of this book provides materials for the youngster as well as parents and other family members. It is important to read or listen to these materials as if one were taking a class with a formal exam. Take notes, decide what approach is best, and implement the ideas involved, always reviewing the responses and benefits. Several treatment goals need to be addressed:

1. Promoting self-esteem

2. Enhancing home and family responsibilities

3. Improving behavioral self-control

4. Managing school and homework responsibilities

5. Developing social skills

6. Enhancing enjoyment of recreational and sports activities

7. Enjoying "going places"

APPROACHES TO ADOLESCENTS

Adolescents with ADHD often experience significant adjustment difficulty because of the unique challenges of their emotional and psychological development. These challenges, in turn, place considerable demands on parents to modify and adapt their approach to their child's treatment. Successful approaches are outlined in terms of:

1. Emotional growth and development

2. Enhancement of family functioning

3. Academic success

4. Medication compliance

ACCOMMODATIONS AND EDUCATIONAL SUPPORT SERVICES

These interventions are provided by school professionals to meet the student's identified weaknesses in terms of academic skills, work production, and social interactions. Some youngsters will also qualify for special educational support services depending on their academic strengths and weaknesses, as determined by formalized psychoeducational testing. Chapter 15, "School Management: The Strategies," provides classroom recommendations for individual teachers in the following areas:

1. Room arrangement

2. Classroom organization

3. Curriculum modification

4. Performance-promoting strategies

5. Behavioral management strategies

6. Strategies for promoting social skills

7. Teacher-parent collaboration

COUNSELING

Family, parenting, or individual counseling may be necessary to assist any or all family members in understanding how ADHD symptoms affect family functioning. Learning coping strategies, and finding solutions to the emotional stress caused by these symptoms can greatly assist the ADHD individual. The requirements for these services differ enormously. Some families will not have a need for counseling services after self-education and management efforts; other families may need intensive psychotherapy. Psychological therapies might include:

1. Individual counseling

2. Group counseling

3. Family counseling

4. Social skills groups

5. Parenting counseling

6. ADHD support groups

7. Coaching

PHARMACOLOGIC INTERVENTIONS

Medication may be indicated as a strategy to facilitate or enhance environmental and behavioral management efforts, allowing the child or adolescent to benefit from the efforts being made by adults on his or her behalf. Medication can enhance the youngster's abilities in terms of behavioral self-regulation and improve day-to-day functioning. Aspects of medical intervention are discussed in later chapters.

Nontraditional Therapies

Nontraditional therapies appear in waves and often gain popularity because of media interest. Many parents are searching for alternatives to medication because of fear of side effects or actual poor tolerance. It is important for parents to understand the history of these therapies, the scientific evidence that exists to support them, and any possible benefits of their use. The therapies discussed include the following:

1. Dietary management

2. Neurotherapy or EEG biofeedback therapy

3. Anti-motion sickness medications

4. Visual or optometric training

Summary

The most successful treatment program will involve an initial self-education process for parents and the diagnosed youngster. Demystifying the symptoms for most families reduces chaos and provides optimism that, given the appropriate diagnosis, successful treatment is possible. An individualized treatment program based on the described differences among individuals with ADHD will lead to improvement. The youngster, his or her family, and the professionals involved must cooperate in designing, implementing, and modifying this personalized treatment program. All adults who are part of the youngster's life should have some level of involvement in the treatment if short- and long-term goals are to be achieved. In truth, for youngsters with ADHD, every waking moment is a therapeutic opportunity to promote their success in the various aspects of their life. Each selected activity will either contribute to these goals or discourage them, based on an awareness of the youngster's needs and a supportive approach. Every day that passes without an active approach to supporting the youngster and promoting success is a lost opportunity never to be regained. Treatment will make a difference. It is never too late! While the intensity of the intervention and the specific strategies used will differ greatly among individuals, improvement will result from virtually any and all sincere, informed efforts.

10

Evaluation and Treatment: Involving the ADHD Youngster

All too often, children or adolescents with suspected ADHD are only minimally involved in their own evaluation and are excluded from the development of a treatment program intended to improve their academic, social, or behavioral profile. Many youngsters have enormous insight into their own difficulties. As a matter of fact, many of them can make their own diagnosis if given the opportunity. Some youngsters will say, "I could get my work done if the other kids didn't make so much noise." Others may say, "I don't understand what the teacher wants me to do when she gives me directions." Still others may say, "I could get my work done if I had a little more time and could work in a quiet place." In addition, when youngsters are asked how they would change their education if they were the teacher or the school principal, they will often have meaningful and productive recommendations.

A 13-year-old boy who was placed in an emotionally disabled class because of his severe behavior problems was asked whether he wanted to attend an academic class. He had not produced any meaningful educational work in at least 2 years. He said that he would like to take a science class but that he would like to take the class from the same teacher twice each day. He said, "You know, I have trouble remembering things if I only hear them once." Given this opportunity, he achieved a B in the class, which ultimately provided direction for future curriculum planning. He knew what was required for him to learn successfully.

Another boy, 10 years old, was asked during an evaluation whether his parents were fair when it came to his chores. He responded:

I had this great idea for my chores. I came up with a ticket system. My parents would give me tickets when I did the chores they wanted and then I could buy the things I wanted like playing Nintendo and going special places.

This youngster with ADHD was unknowingly asking for structure, defined expectations, and a reward system, three of the major principles of home management.

Most youngsters beyond the age of 6 with normal intelligence can understand the origins of, explanations for, and implications of their own attention disorder. While many parents are secretive in discussing their youngster's problem, children are usually quite aware of their own difficulty and experience their own level of frustration. If students are not provided realistic, honest information about their condition, they may assume that there is something more severely wrong with them or that they are truly "bad" or lazy kids. Fully informing youngsters of their developmental weaknesses allows them to participate in planning on their own behalf. This approach also allows youngsters to clarify information that occurs to them after an explanation and to ask relevant questions regarding their condition and future.

In truth, the success of any educational, psychological, or medical therapy clearly involves youngsters' willingness to respond with effort on their own behalf. Youngsters who are unaware of the origin of their problems may well resent an intervention program imposed on them by parents and professionals. Under these circumstances, they may misperceive the intervention's purpose, resist its benefits, and adversely bias the outcome of efforts that might otherwise have been productive.

INTERACTION WITH THE TEACHER

A student can help plan his or her educational intervention successfully if given the opportunity. A private discussion with a sincerely concerned teacher can begin a process of confidential communication that assists both the student and the teacher. Recognition and acknowledgment by the teacher that the student is someone who really tries hard but has limited success because of attention disorder symptoms can quickly enhance the teacher's credibility and the willingness of the student to collaborate. Regularly scheduled reviews can allow for adaptations of the original plan to enhance outcome goals. Positive reinforcement for effort should be an important aspect of any management program.

Special seating plans, a possible private office for work completion, nonverbal cuing, reminders, redirection, strategies, and accommodations in terms of performance measures are examples of topics for discussion with the teacher. All interventions should avoid any embarrassment to the student. One such system might involve the teacher touching the student's right shoulder to reinforce a good effort and touching the left shoulder to indicate that redirection or greater effort is required. Another strategy might involve the teacher looking to the student for a wink or head nod to acknowledge understanding of verbal directions or a shake of the head to indicate that clarification is needed. The opportunity to voluntarily move to a quiet place for work performance is often helpful. Oral test administration or responses (as opposed to the usual written format) might truly reflect a youngster's knowledge. Administration of tests in a quiet atmosphere with extended time allowances might serve the same purpose.

INTERACTION WITH THE PHYSICIAN

The use of medication requires a discussion between the student and the prescribing physician. The youngster must be aware of the purpose of the medication, as well as the personal effort required, in order to benefit. The message that the youngster will deserve the credit for any improvements must be strongly emphasized. There should be ample opportunity for questions about medical therapy. Many students have questions about the safety of the medication, side effects that they are likely to experience, the effects of long-term use, how long they will need to stay on the medication, and who will judge whether the medication has been useful or not. Monitoring issues should be discussed as well. Again, youngsters' input as to the benefit of medication for them should always be solicited and acknowledged. If teacher feedback is sought as part of the monitoring process, the student should be so informed. The dosaging of medication is particularly important to the middle and high school student. The assumption should be made that taking medication at lunch will, at the least, be logistically cumbersome and, at the most, embarrassing. Generally, long-acting medication should be used for this age group. Youngsters as well as their parents should be asked to prioritize their target behaviors in terms of the symptoms of greatest difficulty or desire for improvement. This process will allow for a more appropriate choice of medication and for the most gratifying outcome for all.

BENEFITS

Actively involving youngsters in the development of their treatment plan has several short- and long-term benefits. For example, as mentioned earlier, this honest, respectful approach to dealing with the child's special needs can result in a sense of empowerment and ownership of the process. It also cultivates a therapeutic relationship among the child, the professionals involved, and the parents so that the youngster fully perceives the value of a team approach. A therapeutic relationship that begins with this collaboration will allow for more meaningful communication regarding difficulties as time goes on. There is also an opportunity to engender a sense of pride in the youngster in regard to accomplishments; this inherently increases his or her motivation to succeed. Collaboration can also reduce the concern of many parents regarding the youngster's dependency on medication as a solution to all of life's problems. Youngsters will not believe that medicine has magically cured them; rather, they will perceive it as giving them a sense of independence in confronting life's difficulties.

Enhancing the youngster's participation will also enhance the parents' ability to direct and guide the child as a result of the perceived partnership. This approach will avoid resistance and resentment regarding treatment. Youngsters in their preadolescent years frequently resist medication because they view it as a vehicle for control over them by adults. A collaborative effort helps develop a model for the child to use in future personal and family problem solving. Because the element of resistance is removed, a youngster's ownership of the therapy program allows for a more realistic appraisal of the benefits of various interventions and the need for treatment modification.

Since ADHD is currently perceived as a potential life-span disorder for many individuals, it is essential that the earliest stages of an intervention empower youngsters with a sense of ownership of their treatment program. Ultimately, they will have to make decisions on their own behalf if symptoms persist into later adolescence and adulthood. The time and energy involved in cultivating this level of participation early in treatment have many short- and long-term benefits.

11

Home Management of ADHD

The impact of environmental or behavioral management in the overall treatment of a child or adolescent diagnosed with ADHD is enormous. One family demonstrated this important component even prior to the youngster's evaluation. The parents' observation and discussion with teachers and friends led them to believe that ADHD was an appropriate diagnosis for their 7-year-old son. They began their self-education process prior to his formal assessment. After reading, they decided to actively pursue positive rewards to the greatest extent possible. This program took place 2 weeks before their son's evaluation. At the evaluation, they reported that, based on this simple behavioral strategy, there was at least a 50% improvement in their son's behavioral control, compliance, and apparent desire to please. ADHD did prove to be the correct diagnosis, with their approach being a reasonable first step in treatment.

The preceding scenario highlights behavioral management strategies as the primary treatment for ADHD, especially for the achievement of long-term goals. These long-term goals include maintenance of self-esteem and enhancement of academic functioning, social interaction skills, and communication within the family. These goals can be realized because the environmental or behavioral strategies described in this chapter sustain youngsters' sense of competence and their general sense that they are accepted by the adults who are emotionally most meaningful to them: their parents. The alternative approach of constantly criticizing the youngster and making him or her feel unaccepted places the child at enormous risk for poor self-esteem. Constant discouragement ultimately leads to an inability to develop the realistic, comfortable identity that allows youngsters successful resolution of their adolescent emotional development.

Ten major behavioral themes underlie the specific recommendations described here:

1. Provide structure with flexible boundaries

2. Define expectations regularly

3. Subdivide tasks into their component parts

4. Teach by modeling

5. Communicate in a face-to-face manner

6. Reward effort in addition to outcome

7. Provide positive reinforcement on a frequent basis, even for behaviors that are generally taken for granted

8. Respond to the youngster's behavior not to the child's value as a person

9. Be consistent

10. Accept the child for who he or she is

11. Patience

These principles are translated into specific behavioral management recommendations in terms of seven major categories:

1. Promoting Self-Esteem

2. Home/Family Responsibilities

3. Behavioral Self-Control

4. Homework and School Responsibilities

5. Social Skills

6. Recreational and Sports Involvement

7. "Going Places"

The recommendations provided in this chapter are general in nature. Appropriateness needs to be determined on the basis of individuals' symptom profiles, their strengths and weaknesses, and parenting styles. However, for all parents, getting started is the most important part. Major caretakers should read this chapter together. Some level of agreement as to an approach is quite helpful. Disagreement, especially if it leads to open arguments, is confusing to the youngster and will probably preclude any benefits. If there is disagreement, compromise on one approach for a defined period of time and then modify the approach based on perceived benefit.

Many parents feel that, in implementing these recommendations, they must be "therapists" during all of their waking hours. This is true, but most parents are already spending all day responding to their child's behavior without any desired changes. Often parents find the list of ideas overwhelming; people are busy these days just getting themselves and their families through life. Getting started is critical. Some parents select the most important of the seven categories for their child and start with two or three suggestions. Small successes will grow into larger, more meaningful outcomes.

Parents often underestimate their ability to guide and direct their child's behavior. Often, this unrealistic conclusion is based on their previous experiences in getting the youngster to do what they want. These disappointments are typically based on mislearned behavioral patterns by the child, ineffective or inconsistent messages regarding expected behavior, or excessive focus by parents on negative rather than positive behavior. Even in situations that appear dismal, most youngsters retain a desire to satisfy and meet parental expectations; however, they may lack the skills or strategies to accomplish this goal or be extremely discouraged as a result of previous unsuccessful efforts. The principles of management highlighted earlier and the specific suggestions to follow *can* correct the situation by allowing parents a sense of being able to guide and direct their child and help the child sense that it is possible to please his or her parents. Getting started is essential!

PROMOTING SELF-ESTEEM

- Reward effort rather than always focusing on outcome. A youngster may be making his or her best effort and still not succeed based on parental expectations. Rewarding the effort will promote the child's desire to attempt future endeavors. If the outcome of the task is disappointing, choose one element of the task that reflects effort and reward it. Don't negate a compliment with qualifiers like "But next time. . . ."

- Always begin a new challenging task by defining the expectation in a way that is likely to allow the youngster to succeed in a realistic, age-appropriate fashion. If a youngster is not likely to complete a complicated task, start with a simple requirement that has a high probability of success.

- Highlight the difficulty of a task while expressing confidence in the youngster's ability to complete that task, particularly if the task is new, complex, or potentially difficult or if it involves the youngster's area of weakness. Note and encourage initial efforts.

- Allow for mistakes. Talk about mistakes, even the ones that are made by parents. Equate mistakes with a regular part of the learning process for all individuals. Promote the idea that all individuals make mistakes and but can still comfortably proceed to the next activity or task.

- Help the youngster recognize and identify his emotional reactions to the outcome of any given effort. Help him learn to label the feeling and talk about it, and then accept the feeling as an honest expression. Do not attempt to discount it in an effort to artificially support the youngster. "I thought you did really well" can become a putdown if the youngster realistically knows he did poorly. Children can misinterpret this comment as a parent actually not expecting much from them.

- Involve the youngster in planning an approach to the completion of various tasks and responsibilities. This approach will transmit the message that you believe in the child's planning capabilities and allow for an interchange that will enhance her future planning abilities. Such an approach also decreases impulsive responses to tasks, which often hamper the results of the youngster's efforts.

- Maintain an appropriate perspective regarding school success. School is the work of children and is often perceived by them as a measure of their self-worth. Many youngsters with ADHD and developmental problems are quite challenged by school and, despite their efforts, may experience only marginal success. A youngster's capabilities in other areas must be valued in order to balance the feelings generated by disappointments at school. Realistic goal setting in school for a defined time period can allow youngsters to feel successful in the view of their parents, as well as their own view. This recommendation does not imply that poor school results should be acceptable. All efforts for success at school should continue. However, an emotional balance is necessary.

- Always be aware of your youngster's strengths, and direct and guide her toward activities that express her strengths and allow her the maximum feeling of competence. Recognize that a child who feels unsuccessful will hesitate in trying new things. If success is viewed as probable, provide "strong" encouragement for initial efforts.

HOME RESPONSIBILITIES

- Carefully define expectations for home responsibilities in a practical and specific manner and acquire confirmation from the youngster that he understands the expectations. It will usually be necessary to repeatedly indicate what is expected, even in recurring situations.

- Don't depend on informal recall resulting in a youngster remembering what she is supposed to do, even in terms of daily routines. Write out directions and post them, in addition to expressing verbally what is expected. Often nonverbal reminders or cues are much better received and tolerated by youngsters, especially those in the preadolescent and adolescent age ranges.

- Even if a task is simple, do not assume that the youngster knows how to complete it. As new tasks are introduced, walk the youngster through the task with a combined hands-on and verbal approach. This approach allows him to accomplish a task with parental support before being expected to complete it independently.

- Subdivide tasks into their component parts, especially if the task is lengthy or complicated or has many stages. As the youngster is learning how to do a task, provide directions and reinforcement at each stage to promote her willingness to proceed to the next stage. Reward the result of each stage as the task proceeds.

- Limit the number of expected chores to two or three for any given day. Expectations should include not only completion of the chore but the time line. The best strategy for positive reinforcement is to use a calendar with a notation for each day and each chore. Once a chore is completed in the expected time frame, the youngster receives some type of reinforcement, such as a star or a sticker. If the task is not completed, the youngster loses the opportunity for reinforcement for that chore for that day. If the youngster protests that he was just about to do the chore, simply state that he will have an opportunity to get it done the next day and receive his daily reward. Positive reinforcement on a frequent interval basis is required. It is best to accumulate a defined number of stars and stickers over several days, leading to another reinforcer that grows toward a larger reward, such as an allowance or a special treat at the end of each week. A partial or full allowance can be given to the child based on the extent to which she approached her goals. In addition, the parental response should involve encouragement for the subsequent week and the message of competence for the youngster's ability to achieve the maximum benefits from her efforts. Instructions to create this system are in Chapter 22. The necessary forms are provided in the Appendix.

- Discuss with the entire family the necessary role that all members must play in order for the family and the household to function effectively. Include the ADHD individual as an integral part of this process and provide the same kind of reinforcement program for all youngsters in the family. When the ADHD youngster contributes his share, specifically note how this has helped the family function more efficiently and allowed for more relaxation and recreational time.

BEHAVIORAL SELF-CONTROL

- Attempt to respond to the ADHD child in an emotionally neutral manner, despite your personal level of frustration, disappointment, or anger. This approach has at least three benefits: (a) It models a controlled emotional reaction for the youngster; (b) it avoids conditioning an undesired behavior; and (c) it avoids excessive stimulation of the child, which is often associated with a deterioration of self-control.

- Use "I" messages in identifying how the youngster's behavior is perceived and affects parents. A message such as "It feels to me like you're out of control with your behavior right now" defines your perception and does not criticize the child. It also allows for the opportunity to inform the youngster of your belief in her ability to regain control and your desire to temporarily separate from her while she is out of control and to reengage with her after she settles down. These messages are extremely important as the youngster learns the necessary skills for self-control.

- Balance the necessary response to inappropriate behavior by recognizing and reinforcing appropriate behavior when it occurs, even behavior generally taken for granted. This approach will enhance the youngster's desire for praise and discourage behavior that has often evolved because of the negative attention she has received.

- Consequences (rewards and disciplines) for behaviors must be applied immediately, consistently, unemotionally, and in a predictable manner. ADHD youngsters often require more powerful consequences to change their behavior, follow rules, and sustain consistency in their behavior. Announce consequences for repeated inappropriate behavior to the youngster calmly, during a noncrisis time. Many youngsters will fairly define their own consequence if asked ("What would you do if you were a parent and your child did such and such?"). This role playing may allow for better compliance in terms of negative consequences.

- Introduce new situations to the ADHD youngster by not only defining the content of the activity but defining expectations. If the youngster loses behavioral control in situations that are highly stimulating, introduce those situations gradually while defining behavioral expectations, and provide regular feedback about the youngster's behavioral success during the experience. For some youngsters, highly stimulating experiences should be avoided until they are more capable of coping successfully with these situations.

- Avoid comparing the behavior of an ADHD youngster with that of his peers. The behavioral self-control demonstrated by children often reflects their developmental capability rather than their intent or desire to satisfy adults. A comparison presumes a lack of effort in behaving appropriately, which may not be the major cause of difficulty for the ADHD child.

HOMEWORK/SCHOOL RESPONSIBILITIES

- Recognize that, for youngsters with ADHD, maintaining attention, concentration, and focus on a task is always likely to be more difficult in the evening because of fatigue. Make every effort to ensure that homework is completed after school or as early in the evening as possible.

- Collaborate with the teacher regarding a reasonable amount of homework. It is often better to define the homework expectations by a defined time rather than by the volume of work required. Many youngsters will give their best effort for two or three 20-minute periods of homework separated by rest periods. They could be graded on the work that they've completed rather than what they have not completed. This is an attractive alternative to facing what appears to be an overwhelming amount of homework that could never be completed in one evening. Many teachers will understand the benefits of this approach, especially if the youngster is academically competent.

- Approach every afternoon and evening by assisting the youngster in learning how to plan both recreational and work time. Often a visual depiction (for example, drawing a circle for each hour and dividing that circle into quarter hours) can allow the youngster to fill in her recreational, TV, homework, and telephone time. This approach will ultimately allow her to learn the planning process and time allocation. It will also enhance compliance, since the youngster determined her schedule rather than parents imposing it on her. Model forms for this time management strategy are included in the Appendix.

- Provide a quiet, nondistracting homework environment for all youngsters in the family. It is often helpful to designate a period of time during which no telephone calls are received, the TV is off, and the computer is not available for games.

- Discuss or negotiate with children the desired parental involvement in their homework. Overinvolvement can sometimes backfire, the child's resistance to completing homework being his only means of protesting excessive involvement by parents in this aspect of his life. He may also play out feelings regarding other family issues through homework noncompliance. The age of the child is relevant; more discussion and involvement are needed for older school-aged and adolescent youngsters.

- Develop a system that allows for parental awareness of homework requirements to supplement the youngster's own effort in tracking this information. An assignment book signed off by teachers typically achieves this goal. Every child will require a special reinforcer for maintaining this expectation.

- Request a set of books for home to avoid the youngster not having necessary materials to complete his homework assignments. Various schools will have different policies regarding this request. It is a reasonable accommodation for a student with ADHD. This effort may involve some expense to the family.

- Reward your child's effort in completing her homework and accept her frustration as a reasonable reaction to difficult work rather than assuming that she can approach homework and academic tasks unemotionally. Help her develop strategies for coping with her feelings rather than rejecting her feelings or reflexively reassuring her. "Don't worry about it" is the last thing a worried, frustrated person wants to hear.

- Maintain a regular place for doing homework. A routine can be very useful in avoiding transition problems. The area should be maintained as a workstation as much as possible. Nearby availability of all necessary supplies and materials will avoid the "up and down" transition routine. Good lighting and a neat, nondistracting work surface are helpful.

- Many ADHD youngsters claim to complete their homework better with music playing or the TV on. It is unlikely that the visual and auditory distraction of TV could be helpful. However, music, especially "quiet" music listened to with earphones, might be helpful. Many students indicate that quiet music actually limits their general distractibility (i.e., they have to deal only with one minor distraction). In addition, music is often viewed as the "sacred right" of teenagers and as "necessary" to their lives. If your teenager asks for permission to listen to music while doing homework, consider saying yes; this strategy may help him complete the work, in addition to enhancing parental credibility and collaboration.

- Be certain the youngster has appropriate strategies to approach the homework assignment. Many ADHD youngsters have significant processing strengths and weaknesses that can define the most effective way for them to learn. If there is continuous disappointment or frustration regarding a particular aspect of homework or learning and obtaining information, discuss this issue with the teacher. The teacher's observations regarding learning strengths and weaknesses and possible testing can help in the development of personalized strategies. Some children may be visual learners, while others are auditory learners. There are often relevant differences in short- and long-term memory. Special educators are usually required to translate test results into productive personal strategies. Some experimentation by the student with various approaches is also necessary.

SOCIAL SKILLS

- Recognize that ADHD youngsters often have social difficulties despite their desire for successful interactions. This occurs because of impulsivity, a lack of adequate perception of subtle social cues, an inadvertent violation of social boundaries, associated communication weaknesses, a lack of naturally evolving social skills, an inability to handle self-perceived criticism, a desire to be in control, and difficulty with reciprocity, especially in terms of recognizing the needs of others. For some ADHD youngsters, such difficulties are a major factor in their sense of overall success. These symptoms probably have the same biologic or physiologic origins as core ADHD symptoms such as hyperactivity and inattention. Adults must view these difficulties in this context, not as the behaviors of an indifferent, unconcerned, or willfully inappropriate child.

- Social interactions with a limited number of children are often most successful. It is often helpful to direct the ADHD youngster toward activities that involve fewer children and are more structured. Invite only one or two friends over to play instead of several. Smaller birthday parties and celebrations may be far more enjoyable for everyone.

- Encourage social interaction. Some ADHD children avoid interacting with peers because of previously disappointing experiences. Always create the social experience in a way that is most likely to be successful in terms of encouraging success and future efforts.

- Anticipate possible difficulties regarding social interaction and discuss alternative approaches prior to the experience. Plan to discuss the outcome of such efforts after the experience, with an emphasis on problem-solving benefits rather than criticism of the child for a failed effort.

- Play "what if" with the ADHD child. Review social situations and the effect of the child's actions on others (for example, "How would you feel if that happened to you?"). This will allow her a better perspective of reciprocity and interaction. Role playing in a situation in which the child experiences difficulty can be useful. For example, play basketball and reverse roles. The parent plays the role of the child, and the child plays the role of one of her friends.

- Consider a formal social skills group for ADHD youngsters with interactional difficulties. These groups create communication opportunities for children and allow the children to critique each other with the help of a trained leader so that they can learn from the experience. These approaches can be quite powerful in altering a youngster's approach to other children and in enhancing his or her success.

RECREATIONAL AND SPORTS INVOLVEMENT

- Consider individual rather than team sports for several reasons. First, avoiding team sports reduces the pressure on a youngster who must meet not only his, but a full team's, expectations. Second, individual sports often involve less environmental stimulation and therefore offer the youngster the best possible self-control. Finally, some individual sports, such as martial arts, emphasize self-control, which can be quite therapeutic and helpful to an ADHD youngster.

- Consider the timing of the recreation or sports activity. Be aware of the best and worst times of the youngster's day and try to match the activity to the best time for maximum enjoyment. For example, early evening activities may be difficult because the youngster has worked hard all day regulating his behavior and is fatigued by this time.

- The selection of any recreational or sports activity should be based on a youngster's profile of strengths and weaknesses. Choose activities that the youngster is likely to do well. This is quite important in preserving her self-esteem and balancing some of the disappointments that might occur in academic or other work-related situations.

- Inform activity coordinators of the youngster's ADHD diagnosis so that they can understand him rather than assuming a lack of motivation, desire, or effort to follow directions and comply. Also, provide some clues for successful management so that the initial contact with the youngster can be as positive as possible. The "Let's see if he has a problem before I talk to the instructor" approach is somewhat unfair to both the child and the adult. If all goes well, no harm has occurred. If things don't go well, the instructor can respond therapeutically rather than in a punitive manner. Remember, he or she is part of the child's treatment team.

GOING PLACES

- Always prepare the youngster for a planned outing so that she is aware of the purpose of the outing, the length of time required, the expectations for behavior, and when the next opportunity for "fun" will occur. Some rewards for appropriate behavior should be defined.

- Carefully select those activities that are likely to result in appropriate behavior and avoid those that will create turmoil and stimulate the youngster to the point of reduced self-control. There is no advantage to repeatedly introducing the youngster to situations that are destined to cause him difficulty without providing adaptations or strategies that are likely to improve the situation. Simply confronting the situation will not magically result in improvement.

- If you are attempting an activity that has previously been difficult, prepare the youngster adequately, provide positive reinforcement for appropriate behavior, and be certain that an adult will be available to direct and guide the youngster if he experiences difficulty. A partial reintroduction with a gradual increase in the time or level of participation may allow for ultimate successful adaptation.

- Allow the youngster to participate in selecting places to go when options are available. For example, if two different restaurants would be acceptable, allow the youngster to choose the one she enjoys the most and where she has the best opportunity for appropriate behavior. This will empower the youngster, allow her to learn decision-making skills, and give her a sense of responsibility for appropriate behavior in that setting.

Parents should not be overwhelmed by the suggestions provided here. Select the ones that are most relevant and start with as many or as few as resources allow, but **get started!** It will definitely make a difference in terms of both short- and long-term goals.

12

Special Adolescent Treatment Issues

A dolescents with developmental problems such as ADHD experience significant adjustment difficulties because of the unique challenges of their emotional and psychological development. Even teenagers who have been appropriately diagnosed and treated at an earlier age may experience the same recurring problems. Youngsters who have not yet been identified often experience a complicated pre- and early adolescence because of their lack of success and associated psychological and social traumas throughout their school career.

PREADOLESCENCE

The period of preadolescence, generally between ages 11 and 13, is highlighted by an emotional response of denial. Nothing seems to be important to children in this age range with ADHD. This response aggravates many parents and teachers who believe that young people should be concerned regarding their academic and social progress and interactions in the family. The source of denial relates primarily to the preadolescent's inability to cope with intense feelings that may be generated on a daily basis. Because these youngsters don't have a strategy for dealing with such feelings, they tend to deny the relevance of everything and deal with nothing.

This denial creates an enormous obstacle when preadolescents are asked to actively participate in the management of their identified developmental disorder. They have a strong desire to be like everyone else of the same age, leading them to further deny that they have a problem. Of course, this also leads to a conclusion that since they don't have a problem, no intervention is necessary; as a result, they are unlikely to participate in interventions on their own behalf. This posture, of course, is enormously frustrating for parents and teachers who are trying to help the preadolescent be successful. Conflict between the child's emotional needs and adults' desire for improvement often intensifies the youngster's difficulty, leading to a more complicated struggle that usually further deteriorates his or her level of participation and success.

ADOLESCENCE

Adolescents from 13 to 18 years of age are primarily involved in identity formation. Based on the information acquired through their life experiences, they must define who and what they are through four major tasks:

1. Becoming emancipated from their family

2. Developing their sexual identity

3. Making vocational and academic choices consistent with their perception of their strengths and weaknesses

4. Gaining a sense of altruism or a sense of community

The information used in developing an identity comes from the reactions of both peers and adults to the youngster and his or her interpretation of those responses. The world is like a mirror, with the youngster's image reflected back by life experiences and the responses of others. When adolescents embark on this identity formation, they often have difficulty, especially if they have had to cope with a developmental weakness such as an attention disorder or learning disability. If they are to cultivate a comfortable, realistic, and appropriate identity, they must incorporate information regarding their weaknesses as well as their strengths. This aspect of identity formation is often complicated and confusing, and it leads to a variety of responses by different teenagers based on their personalities, strengths available to balance their weaknesses, emotional comfort prior to their teenage years, and responses of adults and other teenagers to their efforts.

SUGGESTIONS

The following are some specific recommendations for assisting preadolescents and teenagers with ADHD. These recommendations are divided into four categories: (a) emotional growth and development, (b) enhancement of family functioning, (c) academic success, and (d) medication compliance.

Emotional Growth and Development

- Recognize the impact of emotional and psychological developmental issues on a teenager's daily functioning. In this regard, do not presume that the overt behaviors of teenagers actually reflect their feelings. For example, an apparently "lazy" youngster may actually be fearful of trying hard because of the possibility of disappointing results. Making a marginal effort and receiving a poor grade does not involve emotional risk because the adolescent can conclude that he got what he deserved.

- Listen carefully to what the teenager tells you she is feeling and take those feelings seriously. Reflexive reassurances such as "Everything will be fine" or "You know you're not stupid" are not useful and are often viewed as condescending. The teenager's feelings are intense to her and must be dealt with realistically if emotional comfort is to be achieved.

- If possible, attempt to respond to the teenager's behaviors and expressions of feelings in an emotionally calm and neutral fashion. Extreme emotional responses to the youngster are likely to enhance his feeling of being out of control and further complicate the problem. While this is a difficult challenge for most parents, it is necessary because teenagers cannot meet their personal emotional needs and, at the same time, respond to the expressed needs of their parents. While punishment may temporarily discontinue the objectionable behavior, a long-term solution requires empathy, support, and reinforcement for positive efforts, regardless of the level of success.

- Many teenagers and their parents require some type of psychological support and intervention in order to effectively collaborate with each other and develop strategies that will help ease the adolescent's difficulties. Using family therapy as a means of improving family communication and functioning is much more acceptable to teenagers than going to individual therapy, which they perceive as their parents' need to fix them in some way.

Family Functioning

- Prioritize the demands made on the teenager based on their relative importance. For example, most teenagers hold sacred the condition of their bedrooms and their selection of friends, and many will have difficulty complying with restrictions in these areas because of the perceived independence aspects of their personal choices. Negotiation of room status can usually lead to a compromise acceptable to both the teenager and his or her parents. Selection of friends is a very important issue that must be handled sensitively by parents because of the possibility of the parental response aggravating the situation.

- Parents should openly discuss trust and responsibility issues with teenagers. There is often a great deal of misunderstanding as to why parents place restrictions on their teenagers. Youngsters often conclude that parental decisions result from a basic distrust of, or lack of belief in, their sense of responsibility. It is frequently helpful to define specific goals for teenagers that allow them to demonstrate their trustworthiness and responsibility so that they can receive privileges. A vague goal (for example, "You can get a driver's license when you do better in school and can be trusted") is the source of more problems than it solves. Most teenagers believe they've achieved these goals long before their parents come to the same conclusion. Be specific and define goals!

- Parents should attempt to collaborate with teenagers on developing problem-solving skills. Practical, realistic problem solving can relate to parental issues, family needs, or the adolescent's own personal dilemmas. The exercise of collaboration can enhance the teenager's self-esteem in addition to helping him or her learn and experience the process of successful problem solving.

- Parents should negotiate their involvement in a teenager's academic and school efforts. Because youngsters with ADHD often encounter school difficulties, most parents have the natural inclination to remain involved at the level they did when the teenager was younger. Unfortunately, excessive involvement during the adolescent years can lead to resentment and an actual reduction in academic accomplishment. Parents should establish ground rules for negotiation, the first of which is that parents cannot sit idly by and do nothing. Beyond that, both the teenager and the parents should agree on a contract for a defined period of time. The possibilities for a contract are numerous and need to fit individual requirements. Typically, a compromised contract will give a youngster a sense of ownership of the process and lead to an enhanced academic effort. If a negotiated contract is not productive, renegotiation can occur at the conclusion of the defined period of time, allowing for changes in, for example, level of parental involvement.

Enhanced Academic Performance

- Be certain that the teenager is using all possible available technology to support his educational efforts. One solution may be to use a portable tape recorder to tape lectures, allowing the teenager to listen carefully during class and take notes from the tape at his own pace at a later time. The tape recorder may also be used as the teenager attempts to read a chapter in a textbook. He can read aloud the first time he reads the text and play the tape as he reads for a second time, allowing for more meaningful perception of the material. A word processor with a spell and grammar check can be used for written assignments, and a calculator can be used to compensate for time inefficiencies in regard to math calculations.

- Many youngsters complete their homework but never take it to school or hand it in. At times, this occurs because a teenager is unwilling to take the risk of trying and hoping for a good grade only to be regularly disappointed. It is emotionally more comfortable not to hand the work in and get a poor grade than to make an effort toward a good grade with a marginal result. Many teenagers, however, actually forget to take the work to school or to hand it in at the appropriate time. Large neon-colored, translucent envelopes designating a different color for each subject can be used. Immediately after the homework has been completed, it should be enclosed in the envelope, and the envelope should be placed in the teenager's backpack (or another convenient, easy-to-remember place). When he opens the backpack during the day, the large colored envelopes will be apparent, reminding him (it is hoped) to turn in the work.

- Parents can assist adolescents with ADHD be helping them organize an approach to long-term tasks such as major research projects and science experiments. Many ADHD adolescents are overwhelmed by large tasks with multiple steps. It can be helpful to subdivide large tasks into component parts, set shorter goals, and define a time line for completion of each portion. A sense of accomplishment can be achieved for each stage of the project instead of the teenager being overwhelmed by the enormity of the overall endeavor. That sense of success encourages the teenager to begin the next step and work toward completion of the entire project.

- Parents can enhance their teenager's academic efforts by acquiring a second set of books to be kept at home. This allows the teenager to avoid the task of remembering which books are necessary for any given evening. It also avoids the excuse that homework can't be completed because the books were left at school.

- Parents can often assist their teenager by providing tutoring for learning strategies. Most educational programs, including special education, are involved in teaching content material to students. Rarely do students learn strategies for learning. Since all individuals use a profile of strengths and weaknesses to learn successfully, the learning strategies for any one individual must be personalized to that individual profile. Tutors with special education experience can assist teenagers in developing these strategies after tests have defined the student's learning strengths and weaknesses. Such tests should be conducted by skilled professionals who can translate the results into practical recommendations.

- Teenagers should be encouraged to participate in developing the school's approach to meeting their individual educational needs. Often, an educational support plan and accomodations are devised for a student without the student having been asked what approaches might be most useful. Students' participation will allow a sense of ownership of the plan and therefore enhance their willingness to participate.

- Parents can assist their teenager by arranging for test-taking accommodations that may result in enhanced performance. These accommodations might include (a) taking the test in a quiet place, (b) having an extended amount of time to take the test, (c) taking the test verbally instead of in writing, (d) dictating the answers to a scribe, (e) asking teachers to overlook spelling and grammar if the youngster has an associated learning disability, (f) taking a break during the test, (g) having extra time to review the test before handing it in, or (h) even completing the test at home in an open-book fashion. In some instances, students can get test credit by correcting their mistakes after the test has been returned.

- Books on tape should be acquired whenever possible. These tapes can be used while the youngster is reading the academic material, as well as being used independently for review. The combination of visual and auditory input often provides much more meaningful data and information for the student.

- Parents should be aware of signs of stress in teenagers who are making an effort toward academic success. Since ADHD youngsters generally have to work harder than their peers to reach the same level of achievement, they often become stressed by typical educational demands. An occasional break from educational efforts when the teenager appears "stressed out" is legitimate. This response by parents can often enhance their credibility and confirm their empathy for the ADHD teenager's circumstances.

Medication Compliance

■ Pre- and early adolescents typically resist medication for a number of reasons. They are often not clear as to why they are uncomfortable with the medication, and typically they passively noncomply or actively resist, saying they no longer need it. In fact, a variety of reasons usually underlie their sense of discomfort. Demands to take the medication should be avoided. All too often, such situations lead to continued noncompliance because the adolescent refuses to lose the battle regardless of why he or she resisted the medication in the first place. A calm discussion about why the teenager might not want to take the medication, either with parents or the prescribing physician, might identify the specific reason and lead to a resolution of the problem.

Teenagers' most common reasons for medication resistance or noncompliance are:

1. A feeling that they don't actually have an attention problem

2. A belief that they have an attention problem that they can manage on their own

3. An acceptance of the fact that they have an attention problem but a belief that the medication doesn't help

4. Fear of or anxiety about side effects or future effects on their health

5. A feeling that the medication is simply an attempt by their parents and other adults to control them

6. The perception that they are different from their peers because they are taking the medication

7. Embarrassment at taking the medication at school or other kids knowing about it

8. Harassment by a brother or sister because of their need for the medication

9. Undermined sense of competence resulting from parental enthusiasm for the medication (i.e., they feel as though they are being told that they can't handle life without the medication)

10. The fact that they've been taught at home and school to "just say no" to drugs (and they're saying "No!")

Teenagers, when presented these possibilities, will often quite selectively choose the explanation (or several explanations) most relevant for them. This clarification often leads to an educational or problem-solving process that can resolve the resistance and noncompliance.

- If a teenager is taking medication, the parents should avoid uttering the words "Did you take your medicine?" While many teenagers are not able to remember to take their medication on a regular basis and do require reminders, these reminders are often like poison to them. The message the teenagers hear and perceive is "We feel you cannot handle life without the medication." They often resent and resist efforts toward reminders, resulting in considerable noncompliance. This can occur even if the teenager recognizes the benefit of medication. Nonverbal cues or reminders are generally much more helpful and allow the teenager to comfortably take his or her medications. These nonverbal cues might be in the form of posted written reminders, the medication being placed near the bathroom sink or at the breakfast table, or any other form the teenager finds acceptable.

- Parents should encourage teenagers to talk to the prescribing physician regarding their willingness to take medication at school. In general, most teenagers are uncomfortable having to go to the nurse's office at lunch on a daily basis. Administration of medication at school is often associated with noncompliance, especially at the middle school or high school level. Requests should be made to the physician for long-acting medications whenever possible.

- If noncompliance or resistance to medication persists despite the recommendations just described, a demonstration of the continued need and benefit of the medication may be necessary. Many teenagers need proof that they still have attention problems and that the medication helps. They need to be aware that many people observe the benefit of the medication, even though the teenagers themselves don't notice any effect. The medication allows them better initiation and maintenance of attention with less of an intense effort and better consistency.

If these "facts" don't change their minds, then a structured trial off medication for a defined period of time may be necessary. Certain ground rules are important:

The teenagers must self-monitor their performance.
They must be willing to listen to the observations of others.
They must make a significant effort during the trial period.
At the end of the trial period, they must be open to the conclusion of others (or their own conclusion) that there is a noticeable difference in performance, behavior, or emotions off the medication.

This trial period is often best managed and monitored by the prescribing physician. Such an approach can reduce and eventually eliminate the struggle between the parents and the teenager, especially if the teenager resumes taking the medication.

13

Managing Family Stress

M ost families with a youngster with ADHD learn about the youngster's condition in order to provide effective treatments. Under these circumstances, the child's ADHD symptoms generally have only a mild effect on family functioning, with minimal long-term adverse effects. In other families, however, especially before the diagnosis of ADHD is made, the youngster's symptoms may significantly affect all family members. For families who recognize the major impact of their youngster's symptoms on family relationships, the following suggestions are made to reduce this effect. Suggestions address parents' relationship with each other and relationships between siblings.

The first key to reducing family stress is to discuss the youngster's diagnosis openly and in an accepting manner. In many families, the diagnosis is discussed only secretively between parents as if the youngster were guilty of some crime. Most youngsters are fully aware of the symptoms that cause them difficulty and, to some extent, of the impact of those symptoms on others. An open discussion about the youngster's difficulty with his or her ADHD symptoms and the desire of family members to provide assistance is very helpful. This openness allows youngsters to see their symptoms in the appropriate perspective and gives family members a sense that improvement will be forthcoming through their collaborative efforts.

SUGGESTIONS FOR PARENTAL STRESS

- Recognize the source of parental struggles. An initial recognition and acknowledgment of the impact of the ADHD child or adolescent on the marital or parental relationship can begin the process of support. Frequently, struggling exists between parents without the awareness that the ADHD child is the source of the stress. Many parents who have had similar philosophies, in terms of parenting approaches, for their other children become at odds over the ADHD child. Because neither parent's approaches "work," one blames the other and adopts a completely different parenting philosophy. Quickly, one parent becomes the liberal one and the other parent the strict one. The lack of success of either approach polarizes each parent to even further extremes. Both parents become frustrated, angry, and generally discontent and begin arguing about many other issues. A recognition of the source of the struggle can "save" the relationship.

- Support the parenting approach of the other parent completely in instances in which the entire family is present. The worst time to disagree is under the tension of a difficult moment. Disagree and discuss the event later when emotions are reduced and a reasonable conversation is possible. Compromise is always key in any parenting situation. A collaborative parental approach is necessary to achieve a comfortable compromise. In the absence of this perspective, compromise typically involves a destructive sense of winning and losing.

- Accept observations regarding a specific parenting style as being loving and constructive and not as representing criticism or a way to inflict pain. The perfect parent has yet to appear. All parents can improve and benefit from the observations of others. Avoidance of polarization in parenting approaches is extremely important. A negotiated middle position is far better than parents taking their approach to the extreme to balance each other's "mistakes."

- Save personal time for each other. Plan ahead, make a date, or schedule a weekend away. The planning of these "reserved" moments can sustain the relationship between parents and increase their tolerance in times of stress. Most parents must be rigid about completing their plans and not let minor life events cancel them. Obviously, crises may occur that can cause postponements.

- Learn about ADHD together. Share the responsibilities and rewards of successful interventions. Attend support groups together and observe the interaction of other couples. Discuss those observations. All relationships have the potential to change and improve. If overanalysis is tedious for one partner, limit discussion to a briefer time period as the benefits of the effort are realized.

- Define time management as a project with careful planning. Plan to relieve each other for a few moments of relaxation on a regular basis, and don't disappoint your partner when relief is scheduled. Understand that it is okay for different individuals to need more or less relief time. Avoid keeping a balance sheet of who got what; simply provide support.

- Try to maintain a sense of humor. Many situations that are viewed as extremely stressful and painful have an element of humor associated with them. Point out humorous occurrences and enjoy them briefly. This approach will help your children look at the world with a more pleasant perspective.

- Allow yourself the freedom to avoid a difficult situation if you recognize that you are not prepared (in terms of personal resources) to deal with it effectively. No one can be a therapist during all waking hours. However, be cautious not to give the message that you condone inappropriate behavior by totally ignoring it. A minor response indicating your displeasure with the behavior will transmit the appropriate message without requiring an in-depth behavioral reaction.

- Learn to modify or avoid difficult situations in lieu of other family activities that are more predictably enjoyable. The symptoms of a child's ADHD can often turn casual daily activities into stressful life experiences for the entire family. Many parents presume that confronting an area of a child's weakness repeatedly will solve the child's poor functioning in those situations. In fact, the repeated stress of such situations often intensifies the problem. These situations rarely allow for adequate closure so that a positive learning experience can occur.

SIBLING ISSUES

- Identify the unique and special interests or characteristics of each child in the family and design an approach that highlights your interest and concern regarding these characteristics. Some youngsters require encouragement to engage in an activity, but avoid overdoing it; don't encourage them only because you believe the activity is something they should enjoy. Listen carefully to what the youngster wants to do.

- Do not take appropriateness for granted. Siblings will benefit from positive reinforcement even when no special parental response is required. Positive reinforcement is a powerful motivator and will enhance the desire for more favorable responses to their efforts.

- Inform non-ADHD children of the cause of their ADHD sibling's behavior. Do not ask them to become therapists for their sibling; rather, ask them to try to understand the origins of the problem and the efforts being made on their sibling's behalf. This explanation process should not create a burden for siblings or a potential weapon to use against the ADHD youngster.

- Empathize with the feelings of a non-ADHD sibling when difficult situations arise and that child feels victim to a problem he or she is unable to resolve. Listen carefully to the child's feelings and provide reassurance that much effort is being made to improve the situation.

- Encourage all siblings to resolve their interpersonal conflicts using their own resources whenever possible. This approach will allow them to develop an understanding of each other and their personal needs; also, their negative interactions will not become an attention-getting vehicle. Such an approach can lay the foundation for future adult-sibling relationships as well.

- Resist comparison between siblings. All children prefer to believe that they are unique in their own right, and they don't view performing or acting like someone else as a fair expectation. While all children want to be loved, they especially benefit from a personalized expression of that love.

- Behavioral approaches that are initiated specifically for the ADHD child should be generalized to all family members. Limiting TV watching, having children do homework in a quiet place, using behavioral management programs with positive reinforcements, and monitoring behavioral success can improve the performance of all of the children, as well as helping the ADHD child not feel different from his or her siblings.

- When complaints are made about excess attention for the ADHD sibling, be prepared to recall the attention paid to the non-ADHD child and the privileges afforded him or her. If the complaints are realistic, agree and state your intent to improve the situation. A parent's saying "I'm sorry" can often enhance his or her credibility with a distressed child.

- Have non-mealtime family meetings on a regular basis. The focus of these meetings should be problem solving rather than criticism and reprimands. This model will assist all youngsters in the family in learning problem-solving strategies and allow for open communication of feelings often expressed in less productive, emotionally tense situations. All capable family members should rotate as the leader or facilitator of the meeting. The leader determines the initial agenda and controls the flow of conversation. This leader status can enhance the sense of importance of every child. Parents must be willing to "be led" without interfering. Rules of conduct during the meeting should be the initial order of business at the first several meetings. These rules might involve a time limit on individual comments, a banning of "bashing" of any one family member, a no-interruption policy, mandatory attendance, submission of desired topics for discussion in writing before the meeting, a "loving ceremony" of unity at the end (singing a song or holding hands), and procedures for "special or urgent meetings." The decorum of these meetings will often carry over into daily life. Model forms for recording decisions made at family meetings are included in the Appendix.

- Suggest strategies to non-ADHD siblings when they are confronted with the difficult behaviors of their ADHD brother or sister. These strategies are best discussed in noncrisis situations that allow the non-ADHD child to preserve his or her privacy, sense of social boundaries, and freedom of self-expression. Also, help the ADHD child understand the personal needs of his or her non-ADHD siblings. With all children, emphasize how everyone is different, each person having unique strengths, weaknesses, and needs.

14

School Management: The Process

S uccess in school is a critical goal in the overall management of a young-ster with ADHD. Children learn early in their school career to compare their performance with that of their classmates, and lack of success can have important and lasting effects on self-esteem. The teacher's approach to an individual child plays a pivotal role in the child's willingness and effort to achieve academic success.

SCHOOLS AND PARENTS

Requesting and acquiring services for a child through his or her school is often the most frustrating and aggravating activity demanded of parents. Many parents feel helpless when communicating their intense concern about their child's educational progress and feel as though they are receiving absolutely no empathy or assistance from the school. Parents often recall the pain of attending school staffings where they are bombarded by infor-mation and observations about all the things wrong with their child. Many report that they felt the school's presentation was prearranged and scripted so that their input was neither welcomed nor received. They were basically told what would be done to and for their child. Other parents report leaving the staffing feeling criticized for their role in causing their child's problems and for their lack of effectiveness in solving them. Other parents who attend these meetings informed about the school's responsibilities to meet their child's needs are much more satisfied by the school meeting or staffing experience. Preparation seems to be the key.

The relationship between parents and the school does not need to be adversarial. Once school professionals are aware of parents' level of preparation and knowledge regarding their child's rights under the law, they will generally be more accommodating, and a collaborative relationship will evolve. After one or several disconcerting school staffings, many parents decide to bring another informed individual with them to provide advice and consultation during the discussion. Some parents find it useful to tape record the meeting for a subsequent review of the discussion, as well as conclusions and decisions. If the tone of a meeting is too negative, parents may ask for a description of the child's strengths within the school setting. This request has three potential benefits:

1. It modifies the tone of the meeting, participants recognizing that all youngsters have strengths in addition to their weaknesses.

2. It reassures the parents that school professionals truly understand their child.

3. It is likely to result in educational, behavioral, and social strategies that can be used to improve the student's current level of functioning.

Many parents with ADHD children are hesitant regarding informing the teacher and other school personnel about their child's diagnosis. The typical fear is that the diagnosis will define the teacher's expectations for their child and that the teacher will perceive the child only in stereotypical ADHD terms. Parents are concerned that teachers, under these circumstances, may have minimal expectations for the child's performance and may understimulate or inadequately challenge the student. They are also concerned that the diagnosis will not remain confidential, becoming a topic of conversation in the teacher's lounge or among students.

While all of these concerns may be realistic with some teachers and in some school circumstances, the need for educational accommodations usually predominates. The necessity for educational accommodation as an integral aspect of overall management is clinically documented on a regular basis. If labeling and intervention ensure success, maintain motivation, and preserve self-esteem, they are worthwhile. For parents who are particularly sensitive, confidentiality can be requested from individual teachers as long as informal arrangements remain the mechanism for acquiring services.

MECHANISMS FOR GETTING HELP

Students with ADHD can receive help through three mechanisms:

Informal arrangements with the classroom teacher
A formal process required by Section 504 of the 1973 Federal Rehabilitation
    Act
Special education services through the Individuals with Disabilities Education Act

Informal Arrangements

Informal arrangements typically are a result of the teacher, the student, and the student's family meeting to determine the accommodations that would be most helpful. Parents generally make recommendations from their personal experience or their self-education process. Ideally, a list of possible accommodations (such as those described in this chapter) should be reviewed by the parents and the student prior to meeting with the teacher. From this extensive list, three or four items should be selected that have the potential of being most helpful. The teacher should then be asked to implement these specific ideas. The teacher may also bring creative ideas from his or her previous teaching experience and education. This meeting should blend these various accommodation opportunities into a time-limited plan that will be reasonable for the teacher and acceptable to the student. Subsequent meetings can be scheduled to review progress and the success of the implemented accommodations. Appropriate adaptations and modifications can be made at that time.

This approach has enormous potential to encourage active collaboration between the student and his or her teacher. For many students, this may be the first time that a teacher has expressed belief in them as being capable of achieving success and the willingness to participate on their behalf. The process also acknowledges that the student, despite periodic appearances, really does care about his or her school success and is willing to make a reasonable effort to achieve that success. The teacher and the parents are brought together as partners in directing and guiding the student's educational efforts. This partnership implies a mutually agreed, shared responsibility for the youngster's success and defines the role of each party in working toward that goal. The process also allows for sharing frustrations rather than pointing fingers. Joy and a sense of accomplishment can be shared when things go well.

Many parents report seeking informal arrangements with a particular classroom teacher only to find that the teacher has a negative attitude about the existence of ADHD, claims to have too many students to serve any one student individually, states that he or she does not have experience with ADHD and cannot be expected to serve the youngster's needs, or is over-worked and underpaid and can't be bothered. These reactions sometimes occur if parents approach teachers with demands of a detailed, complicated, time-consuming approach to their child's needs. Under these circumstances, many teachers will become defensive and resistant. For this reason, the approach to most teachers should be one of expressing the student's need for help and determining the teacher's role in a broader, comprehensive intervention program. Rather than making demands, it is often useful to inform the teacher of strategies useful in the past. It is always best to ask for a few accommodations with a high level of probable success rather than to overwhelm a teacher with enormous demands that are so complicated that no strategies are implemented. If a softened, simplified, and modified approach does not improve the situation, then parents must decide on the next course of action.

Section 504

Typically, speaking with the school counselor or principal represents the next option available to parents. Again, these conversations should highlight the needs of the child rather than anger at the uncooperative teacher. Most often parents will then be directed to the process, within the school, for implementing Section 504 provisions. If parents experience further resistance or a response that denies the school's responsibility to a student with ADHD, they should indicate their awareness of their child's rights under Section 504. If the school counselor or principal appears unfamiliar with this legislation, parents should then allow them a brief period of time to consult with other administrators within their district regarding their legal requirement to serve the youngster.

Section 504 of the Federal Rehabilitation Act, passed in 1973, stipulates that institutions receiving federal dollars must serve students with any of a number of various medical conditions. ADHD is one of those conditions. Various schools have implemented this responsibility quite differently. Many schools rely upon an informal relationship among the student, the student's parents, and individual teachers. Other schools handle their Section 504 responsibilities more formally by developing what is typically called a "504 Student Accommodation Plan."

A formal 504 Student Accommodation Plan process generally involves the referral of the student to a student review team that typically includes a 504 coordinator, the student's academic counselor, the classroom teacher, and a resource individual or expert on ADHD. The 504 plan is developed in conjunction with the parents and approved for implementation. Strategies and measurable outcome goals are defined. The roles of the student, teachers, and parents are also defined. This approach is particularly desirable if the individual teacher has not had experience with the management of ADHD or is resistant to accommodating to a student's needs. It is also helpful when multiple teachers are involved and a coordinated effort is required, particularly at the junior high and high school levels. Typically, the 504 plan is reviewed on an annual basis. At that point, modifications and adaptations based on the success of the previous plan and the student's current needs are made.

Other administrative arrangements may be appropriate for accommodations, depending on the specific needs of the student and the resources available within the school. A school psychologist or counselor or a student nurse might serve as a consultant to an individual teacher, on an informal basis, regarding the management of a particular ADHD student. This model is most effective if the teacher is interested in assisting a student but lacks the necessary education or personal experience. Current teachers often contact previous ones to determine successful strategies that can be implemented in the classroom. Periodic advice can be sought by the classroom teacher from any of these school resources when new challenges or difficult situations exist and solutions are not forthcoming.

Special Education

Students may receive services under the Individuals with Disabilities Education Act, or what is commonly known as "special education." These services may be obtained for the ADHD youngster via a number of different categories. If the student has coexisting learning disabilities, he or she may qualify as a student with specific learning disabilities. If a student's behavior is so serious a problem that he or she cannot be managed in a regular classroom, he or she may qualify as having a serious emotional disturbance. A mentally retarded student with significant attention disorder symptoms may qualify under the Mental Retardation category. Most commonly, ADHD students qualify for special education in the "other health impaired" category. A student may qualify under this category if ADHD impairs and adversely affects educational performance to a significant degree and if the resources of regular education are determined to be inadequate to serve the student's needs.

Services typically provided through special education are similar to the accommodations provided under Section 504. In addition, the resources of a special education teacher become available through a pull-out program involving the student leaving the regular classroom for a scheduled period of time during each week and going to a resource room or learning center for assistance. This support may be provided on a one-to-one basis but more commonly occurs in a situation involving three or four students and one teacher. Many schools have modified their program so that the special education teacher goes into the regular classroom and serves a few students with similar problems simultaneously while usual classroom activities continue. This integrative or inclusion model of services is currently being studied to determine its relative value in comparison with the more traditional resource room model. Cost-effectiveness is also a concern in evaluating this approach.

The content of the individualized work with the ADHD student should be determined by the student's educational and behavioral needs. Additional services might be provided by a school counselor in the form of group counseling. Typically, group counseling has the goals of advancing the social interactional skills of students, helping them to better understand the underlying causes of their difficulties, and assisting them in forming strategies that will enhance their overall functioning and performance.

Individualized Education Plans

The Individuals with Disabilities Education Act requires the development of an individualized educational plan (IEP). The IEP, a formal contract between the local school district and the parents, defines specific services that will be provided to the student. The IEP is generated at a meeting attended by a representative of the school (other than the child's teacher) who is qualified to provide or supervise the provision of special education services. The child's teacher should be present as well. Prior to a child being placed in special education, this will generally be the regular classroom teacher. After placement, both the regular classroom teacher and the special education teacher should attend. Parents must be present and are expected to participate in the creation of the IEP, along with school professionals. The student may attend when appropriate, depending on age, level of understanding, and emotional and behavioral status. One or several members of the evaluation team will often be present, and other individuals can attend as the need arises.

The IEP must include:

1. The child's present educational level, which is typically measured annually

2. Annual goals

3. Short-term goals

4. Specifically defined special education and related services

5. The duration of the plan (typically 1 year)

6. The requirement for reevaluations and annual reviews

Parents may request an IEP meeting prior to the annual scheduled meeting if their child is not progressing satisfactorily or if the current IEP is not being implemented as anticipated. It is extremely important for parents to be aware of their child's rights, as well as their own rights, under the Individuals With Disabilities Education Act. As with Section 504, it is important to be aware of students' rights when interacting with the school. Such information is generally available through state and national advocacy groups (see the Information Resources section). Lay and professional educational advocates are available on a voluntary or fee-for-service basis in many communities; these individuals can interpret the laws for parents, as well as being actively involved in communication with the school. The names of these persons often can be obtained by talking with other parents or the leaders of local ADHD parent groups or Learning Disability Association organizations.

Parents are not obligated to sign 504 plans or IEPs at the time of their creation and/or presentation. If a level of discomfort exists regarding the appropriateness or adequacy of the proposed plan, parents can take the necessary time to think about it or consult with an outside resource regarding modifications or an alternative proposal. While this approach may delay implementation, the best outcome can be expected only if the plan is appropriate and reflects the child's needs. Such time is typically well spent, since the plan is likely to be in force for a full academic or calendar year.

If the collaborative effort between parents and the school to support the needs of the student fails, there are well-defined legal remedies for parents. These remedies should be considered when all other efforts have failed. Information on specific legal procedures available to support the rights of students and their families can be obtained through the national advocacy organizations listed in the Information Resources section. Advice can be sought from state offices of the Center for Law in the Public Interest, which often has a division dedicated strictly to educational law and student rights.

15

School Management: The Strategies

When ADHD symptoms adversely affect academic performance and success, educational accommodations will be necessary. The most appropriate and effective strategies will vary from student to student. In this chapter, possible accommodations are presented in the following categories:

Room arrangement
Classroom organization
Curriculum modification
Performance-promoting strategies
Behavioral management strategies
Strategies promoting social skills
Teacher-parent collaboration

These specific teacher recommendations should be reviewed with the ADHD youngster. Select three to five of the most useful and acceptable ideas and share them during a parent-teacher meeting. A give-and-take discussion about which ideas the parents and student believe will be helpful and which the teacher feels she or he can implement can lead to an initial approach to the child's needs. Providing too many desired accommodations may overwhelm even the most cooperative teachers and lead to less enthusiasm and interest on their part.

ROOM ARRANGEMENTS

- Seat the student close to the teacher's desk, but be certain that he or she perceives this as an opportunity rather than a punishment.

- Attempt to seat the child adjacent to organized, productive classmates for modeling purposes.

- If possible, increase the space between the student's desk and classmates.

- Reduce the amount of distracting visual stimuli close to the child's work area.

- In collaboration with the student, provide a private, nondistracting "office" area where, periodically, he can voluntarily place himself for greater work production efficiency.

- Model desk organization by keeping the your desk and material orderly.

- Identify and clearly designate an area for turning in work in the typical walking path of the child. Make it easy to remember to turn in work. While most teachers expect students to initiate this process, youngsters with ADHD actually may forget. They also may be reluctant to "take a risk" and be graded (criticized) because of previous disappointing experiences.

- Use nonverbal cues as reminders for classroom expectations as much as possible. A reminder note placed on students' desks each morning might assist them in turning in homework or remind them of the preparation steps for an assignment. Parents will often supply the required materials.

- Allow for a predetermined area where the student can get up and move about briefly during seatwork without disturbing classmates.

CLASSROOM ORGANIZATION

- Display classroom rules for all students to review.

- Post the daily routine and schedule, attempting to maintain a defined order of subjects and activities. Provide a copy of this schedule near the student's desk.

- Allow time for the student to organize herself during transitions to a new activity or learning experience.

- Announce transitions in advance of their occurrence, using a quiet countdown procedure with transition directions as appropriate.

- Alternate activities requiring a high level of concentration with those that are more relaxed.

- Plan most intense academic subjects and activities in the morning hours, when most students are more alert and attentive and less fatigued.

- Negotiate with the student a set of nonverbal cues that will assist him in following routines required for classroom success. For example, a touch on the right shoulder might reinforce an appropriate effort, while a left shoulder touch would remind the student that he ought to redirect his attention to the task at hand. Positive reinforcement must be used as frequently as (or more frequently than) redirection cues.

CURRICULUM MODIFICATION

- Reduce the amount or volume of work required to fully complete assignments.

- Allow an extended period of time for completion of work, especially long-term or complicated projects.

- At the initiation of a new learning experience, allow for a lower accuracy rate and elevate expectations with time.

- Modify homework expectations, focusing on effort rather than absolute work production. Determine with parents a reasonable homework time commitment and grade the student on what he has completed during that time rather than on what he did not finish. Many ADHD students will complete as much work in this defined period of time as they would during a long, tedious, seemingly endless evening of homework.

- Modify tasks that involve significant inherent distractions. For example, math work sheets with 50 problems on a single page create 49 distractions whenever the student attempts a single problem. Fewer items on the page or a cardboard cutout overlay can allow better focus on a single problem at a time.

- Subdivide multistage or complicated tasks into their component parts so that the student can complete one piece successfully and be reinforced before moving on to the next step.

- Use lined or graph paper to enhance visual organization for all writing assignments.

- Track incomplete work and periodically (weekly) provide reminders to the student and her family. Reminders should redefine the task and specify the due date with possible extension options.

- For complicated or lengthy tasks, present only a portion of the total assignment at a time.

- Include organizational and study skill strategies as a curriculum presentation for all students, and include a special adaptation for the ADHD student. For example, determination of the necessary steps in completing the assignment should occur before the actual project work is begun.

PERFORMANCE-PROMOTING STRATEGIES

- Encourage the use of tape recorders, computers, word processors, calculators, and other technological advances when potentially beneficial. For example, if a student has difficulty taking notes during a lecture-type presentation, he could tape record the lecture while listening carefully. He can then take notes at home while listening to the lecture at his own pace.

- Provide verbal and nonverbal positive reinforcement for effort and work production on a frequent basis.

- When scoring homework assignments or tests, mark the correct items rather than the incorrect responses. While this approach may seem trivial, highlighting the weaknesses of struggling students can add to their discouragement.

- Simplify presentations of directions and make them available in a multisensory format (verbal and visual). Make direct eye contact when presenting directions.

- Develop a system with the student so that she can nonverbally acknowledge her adequate receipt and understanding of directions. If the acknowledgment does not occur, calmly repeat the directions for the entire class or provide direct guidance for the ADHD student.

- Ensure that the student is clear regarding homework assignments and has taken the appropriate materials home (or, if possible, has a second set of books at home).

- Consider an end-of-the-day "buddy" system for all students in which the students, in pairs, assist each other in concluding the day's work, preparing for homework, and reviewing requirements for the next day's work. The ADHD student can be paired with an organized "helping" classmate by design without the appearance that the system is designed exclusively for him.

- Consider elevating the ADHD student's self-esteem by allowing her to tutor a classmate with lesser skills in a particular area or tutoring in a lower grade.

- Modify testing protocols to allow for:

  Extended or untimed tests
  Oral test taking
  Having questions read to the student if he or she has poor reading skills
  Test taking in a quiet, nondistracting environment
  Use of limited notes or book material to compensate for poor memory
  Use of a word processor or calculator to compensate for weaknesses in particular academic areas
  Questions about material that has been specially highlighted in teaching presentations

- Teach students to use a color coding system while reading and studying written material (i.e., they can highlight different types of information, such as names, dates, and definitions, in different colors).

- Offer solutions for completing unfinished work in a time-efficient but meaningful manner so that the student can experience a sense of accomplishment. This approach might involve prioritizing incomplete work, excusing some repetitive assignments, or creating a time line for being "caught up." The system can be implemented weekly or biweekly so that the student never falls too far behind.

- Reward efforts toward successful task completion as well as production or completion of work. Many students feel as though they have tried quite hard to complete the work despite falling short of the assignment expectation. A lack of acknowledgment of this effort is quite discouraging and can create a major disincentive for future efforts.

BEHAVIORAL MANAGEMENT STRATEGIES

- Clearly define behavioral expectations and consequences of inappropriate behavior early in the school year and periodically review these guidelines with all students.

- Always attempt to provide positive reinforcers for appropriate behaviors. Such reinforcers are always more potent motivators than negative consequences.

- Rewards for appropriate behavioral effort should be frequent, and an attempt should be made to use reinforcers most meaningful for the particular student. Reinforcers might include one-to-one attention, verbal praise, awarding of special classroom responsibilities, extra free time, increased computer time, or reduction in work demands.

- Predetermine consequences of behavior in collaboration with the student during a private meeting at which concerns can be discussed calmly without excessive emotions. This preparation may avoid an overreaction by the student when consequences are implemented.

- Avoid lengthy verbal interchanges regarding inappropriate or disruptive behavior and proceed with redirection or consequences calmly, directly, and firmly.

- Avoid humiliation and embarrassment. ADHD students are already sensitized to their differences and often suffer self-esteem problems even at the earliest grades. Whenever possible, infractions and consequences should be discussed privately and confidentially.

- Provide problem-solving alternatives to the student for situations that evoke inappropriate and disruptive behavior. A suggestion of an alternative behavioral response to a specific situation might allow for better behavioral choices the next time the situation occurs. It is important for the tone of this discussion to be calm and interactive rather than reprimanding.

- Preempt "high-risk" situations (i.e., situations that typically trigger inadequate behavioral regulation) by describing anticipated events and rehearsing responses. The student may decide not to participate if he feels unprepared to cope effectively. A successful partial or abbreviated experience may ultimately expand to fuller, rewarding participation.

- Do not threaten students with improbable consequences out of frustration or exasperation.

- Preplan voluntary, self-regulating time-out locations outside the classroom for episodes that escalate out of control. The student may elect to use this strategy voluntarily or may be firmly directed to the location by the teacher.

STRATEGIES PROMOTING SOCIAL SKILLS

- Resolve interactional difficulties by interpreting to the student why his behavior upsets others and providing suggestions for how he can solve the problem.

- Select a popular student to serve as a partner for the ADHD student in buddy sessions, unstructured activities, and transitional situations.

- Avoid asking classmates to understand the ADHD student and become a "therapist" for her. This often places the ADHD child in a socially vulnerable situation, making her the target of taunting and insulting remarks.

- Suggest that the school counselor or psychologist create a social skills group that would meet regularly to discuss, model, and role play appropriate interactional skills.

- Provide accommodations to the ADHD student but try to avoid a situation in which the student appears too privileged. Accommodation to the needs of the ADHD student is an essential aspect of his treatment; however, other students may resent his status. Many accommodations can be accomplished discreetly. For example, a student may take a scheduled test with the whole class but retake the test later or at home for actual scoring and credit.

- Facilitate problem solving between students without assuming the role of referee or judge.

TEACHER-PARENT COMMUNICATION

- Initiate or agree to schedule a meeting prior to or early in the school year in which you share concerns with parents, allow parents to indicate their expectations, and describe your personal experiences, resources, and time availability in terms of serving their ADHD child.

- Schedule a monthly session with parents regularly to review progress and identify areas of concern.

- Provide parents with routine feedback, via an assignment book, regarding unfinished work, effort, and behavioral ratings.

- Solve problems collaboratively by means of parents' experience from previous school years and from home.

- Provide feedback, upon request, about the benefits and/or side effects of medical interventions.

- If input is not requested and concerns exist regarding the inadequacy of a medication, compliance issues, or perceived side effects, ask for the opportunity to communicate with the prescribing doctor directly or through the parents. If the doctor seems unresponsive, ask permission from the parents to submit a report to the doctor for the child's medical record. Then suggest that the parents make an appointment with the doctor specifically to discuss the report.

When the request is made for teachers to implement any of these strategies, it is important to emphasize their critical role in the overall management of the child with ADHD. Highlighting the benefits of similar approaches at home will provide encouragement to the teacher. Always emphasize the "team" approach.

16

Psychological Therapies

Youngsters with ADHD are at particular risk for life experiences that are socially and emotionally traumatizing. Many of these youngsters, however, do extremely well. The best psychological status can be expected if the child is diagnosed at the earliest possible age and a treatment strategy begun. Adaptation and modification of the youngster's management program based on age, emotional development, and reaction to life experiences can sustain that probable positive emotional outcome. Most youngsters diagnosed somewhat later demonstrate enormous emotional resilience once the cause of their difficulty is identified, the chaos in their lives is reduced, and a treatment program is initiated. Even teenagers, particularly if they have been emotionally supported by their families, can show resilience despite years of confusion, disappointment, and frustration. Early identification and treatment, therefore, serve the major purpose of sustaining individuals' self-esteem despite their weaknesses.

However, many ADHD youngsters remain susceptible to emotional difficulties as a result of delayed diagnosis, ineffective and inconsistent treatment, insensitive peers and adults, lack of a comprehensive individualized treatment program, and the youngsters' own sensitive temperament.

Many professionals and parents believe that the most important long-term goal for children and adolescents with ADHD is maintenance and preservation of self-esteem. Children with ADHD are particularly at risk of feeling poorly about themselves. Because symptoms occur in virtually all situations, these children continually receive negative messages about themselves, quite often at a very young age. For example, an extremely hyperactive 3- or 4-year-old who has been excluded from one or several preschools, not been allowed in the grandparents' home, and been told to stay away from the neighbor's dog may begin to feel quite sad or may display a significant amount of anger. Even at this young age, ADHD children's belief in their ability to be successful in the world is often wavering. Because of their sadness, anger, and frustration, they may develop behavioral symptoms that further reduce people's tolerance of them, resulting in their exclusion from certain situations.

Virtually all kindergarten students are inquisitive and are anxious to learn unless they have received negative messages regarding their competence. If they begin kindergarten with excitement and enthusiasm but receive messages of social unacceptability and performance inadequacy, they will soon begin to wonder whether they are okay. If this pattern continues through first grade, they may quickly alter their self-perception and conclude that they will not ever be able to succeed in school or get along successfully with other students. Furthermore, they may respond to frustration, confusion, and disappointment with inappropriate behavior directed at teachers, peers, and often family members.

EVALUATION

During evaluation, adolescents, particularly those not previously diagnosed as having a developmental problem such as a learning disability or ADHD, will often relate stories regarding their past with an astonishing memory. They often remember single episodes early in their school career that biased their approach to school forever. One teenager related an experience in third grade when his apparently well-meaning teacher had him stand up during class. She told the rest of the class to point their finger at him whenever he wasn't paying attention. The embarrassment and resentment were overwhelming. At that moment in time, he concluded he would never be successful in school and decided to make minimal effort toward academic achievement. Of course, that decision further complicated his life because all of the adults around him concluded that he was simply being lazy and responded with punishment.

A college student told of an experience with her fourth-grade teacher. The teacher, who became aware of the young student's difficulty paying attention, decided on an intervention. She appropriately decided to use nonverbal cues to help this student remain on task. Unfortunately, she told the student that she would pull on her pigtails whenever she wasn't paying attention. Because of the student's temperament, she became extremely anxious regarding this possibility. Her anxiety reduced her performance significantly. She had this same teacher for 2 years but never told anyone of the source of her anxiety. Two years of her school career were destroyed, reducing her foundation of academic skills as she moved forward in her school career. She also was left with a general sense of anxiety regarding her ability to be successful at school and uncertainty regarding her school as a safe place for her.

A common phenomenon for children and adolescents with developmental problems and/or ADHD is completing homework without turning it in. Certainly, the ADHD characteristics of poor organizational skills, poor short-term memory, and impulsivity may contribute to this problem. However, more often students, especially teenagers, will explain that this symptom is the result of years of criticism of their work. At some point in time, they make the decision, either because of their own observations or because of events such as those described earlier, that they are not going to be able to be a successful student. Previous efforts at doing well in school typically led to agonizing frustration and repeated disappointments.

Such discouraging experiences strongly affect students' self-esteem and sense of competence. Eventually, often unconsciously, they make the decision to emotionally protect themselves. Because they are basically "good kids," they show up for class and demonstrate a reasonable level of interest; however, they are well known for doing only as much as they have to. Their need to emotionally protect themselves is intense. They unconsciously conclude that if they do not hand in their work or hand it in late, they will receive a justified poor grade. This poor grade does not result in any emotional pain because they never made the effort to succeed in the first place.

If, however, they make the effort with the hope of achieving some level of success, they place themselves at risk for further criticism, poor grades, and, therefore, more frustration, anguish, disappointment, and discouragement. Completing their homework but not turning it in eliminates the possibility of emotional pain. Unfortunately, such a self-protective emotional strategy leads to its own set of complicated life experiences, resulting in punishment, parental anger, formal school discipline, and personal restrictions. Of course, these students' effort to emotionally protect themselves actually leads to more emotional trauma, further worsening their self-esteem.

THERAPY

Because of these experiences and the emotional consequences of ADHD-related weaknesses, psychological therapies are often a critical aspect of the ADHD youngster's overall treatment program. Generally, with each passing year the requirement for psychological intervention increases. Over time, the number of emotionally negative experiences accumulates, often intensifying emotional and psychological feelings and escalating the behavioral responses to those feelings. Virtually all older school-aged children, pre-adolescents, and adolescents will require some specific attention to their psychological needs in order to guarantee successful management of their underlying ADHD.

In addition, the presence of coexisting or secondary psychological diagnoses such as oppositional defiant disorder, mood disorder, anxiety, depression, and conduct disorder will lead to the necessity for specific psychological therapies. Some of these coexisting diagnoses are amenable to medical intervention (as described later in this book); however, psychological therapies are typically useful and often necessary.

Approximately a quarter of youngsters with ADHD exhibit significant difficulty getting along with classmates, neighborhood friends, and relatives. Some possible causes of this problem:

Poor sensitivity to subtle verbal and nonverbal social cues
General social misperception or a lack of appreciation of social situations
Lack of a sense of personal boundaries and space and inadvertent intrusion
    into others' space
Verbal and behavioral impulsivity
A need to be "in control" or bossy in peer play
Attempts to overcompensate for poor self-esteem
Unawareness of social "rules"
Antagonism or anger resulting from lack of acceptance by peers
Associated language processing weaknesses

These social skills issues often require therapeutic intervention.

The psychological needs of and appropriate treatments for ADHD children and adolescents vary enormously depending on several factors:

Age
Severity of symptoms
Age at diagnosis and success of interventions
Extent of disruption caused by symptoms
Severity of functional impairment
The family's social and emotional integrity or support
Level of impairment in terms of social interactions
The family's general acceptance or rejection of the child
Strengths available to balance weaknesses
Emotional resilience
Temperamental profile

A variety of psychological therapies are available and should be considered on the basis of these characteristics.

Social Skills Groups

In social skills groups, children have the opportunity to interact with peers in a structured manner, where the children critique each other's behavior. A trained leader is necessary if the experience is to be meaningful and productive. Role playing, videotaped interactions, and "feelings identification" are some of the strategies used. Through analysis and discussion of each other's behaviors, youngsters can learn new ways of listening, watching, and responding.

Individual Therapy

Individual therapy with a professional who understands child development, school and family systems, and ADHD can be helpful. Such therapy has several goals:

- To help youngsters understand the origin of feelings resulting from their ADHD symptoms and to appreciate the effect of these symptoms on others

- To help youngsters appreciate the effect of their feelings on their behavior and effort at home, in school, and with peers

- To help youngsters learn coping strategies that allow for alternative ways to express their feelings in a more appropriate and acceptable manner

- To help youngsters learn self-monitoring techniques to heighten their awareness of how their behavior affects others

- To help youngsters learn ways to resolve stress and conflict successfully

Family Therapy

Family therapy, involving various combination of family members, including siblings, can be another helpful strategy. The goal of this approach might be to enhance communication between family members through the use of listening techniques, conflict resolution strategies, contract negotiation, therapeutic interruption of escalating verbal interactions, boundary clarification, interpretation of feelings, nonverbal communication techniques, "I" messages, role definition, and other intervention techniques. Siblings can be assisted in understanding the origins of the affected sibling's behavior and effective techniques to minimize conflict.

Parent Training

Parent training can assist parents in learning strategies that promote appropriate behavioral regulation, responsibility, and compliance. Extended family members or others who have significant caretaking responsibilities or regular contact should be involved so that expectations and behavioral management approaches will be consistent. Behavioral and environmental management goals can often be met through reading and watching videotapes as well as consultation between parents and teachers. In addition, many parents can benefit from parenting groups and counseling in terms of developing the most effective strategies to guide their child.

ADHD Support Groups

ADHD support groups can be helpful to most parents. These groups serve educational goals by inviting experts or representatives from community organizations to speak. Emotional support is provided by:

1. Discussion of common concerns

2. Experienced parents sharing their personal stories and successful outcomes

3. Group problem solving

4. Interactions with adults who understand the demands on parents of youngsters with ADHD

Experienced parents can help guide others to helpful community professionals and organizations (and also indicate the ones to avoid). Strategies to deal successfully with school systems are often shared. The experience of socializing with ADHD children in a setting where they are "accepted" may be unique and pleasant. Many parents find their support group involvement and the friendships that emerge to be an extremely important part of their lives. Friendship with other adults who are willing to provide support, sensitive criticism, and suggestions—and who are willing to modify their social plans and activities based on the needs of your ADHD youngster—is welcome for many parents. The Information Resources section lists national organizations that can provide names of contact persons for support groups in most communities or geographical areas.

Coaching

Coaching is a relatively new therapeutic term for an old human habit. All of us seek assistance in areas in which we feel particularly weak or lack necessary skills. A coach lends support to an individual with ADHD on either a formal or informal basis. Many laypeople and professionals are now finding that assisting others with these services can be very gratifying. A coach may help individuals enhance skills required to organize their life and daily activities, establish priorities, arrange efficient schedules, manage finances, and set short- or long-term goals. These activities involve the short-term goal of managing one's life as effectively as possible. The long-term goal is to learn these strategies so that one can competently, efficiently, and successfully manage one's daily life.

17

Principles of Medical Intervention

Medication has the potential to be helpful in the treatment of ADHD because of the presumed underlying biochemical or neurotransmitter variations that appear to cause ADHD symptoms. While these variations have not been specifically proven and cannot be clinically measured in any one individual, scientific studies have provided useful information. These studies, along with experience with medications, have allowed physicians to correlate symptoms with possible neurotransmitter variations. Medication can, artificially and temporarily, "fix," change, or correct these variations.

Medication effects can provide the opportunity for individuals to change their behavior and promote their performance. The medication does not inherently create these improvements; there is no magic involved. The individual must make the effort to behave and perform in a specific manner, the neurotransmitter changes allowing that effort to be more successful.

The correlation between symptoms and neurotransmitters is not an exact science. However, some suggestion regarding the best initial choice of medication can result from this knowledge. Responses to medication can provide insight as to underlying neurotransmitter variations. This experience can assist in the selection of alternative or additional medications.

Treatment with medication has become the most common intervention for ADHD in the United States. Unfortunately, medication is often used as the only treatment, a practice that commonly leads to disappointing long-term outcomes. The most appropriate role for medication is as a **facilitator** for behavior management, school accommodations, and psychological therapies. Medication can allow individuals to be more attentive and to have better control over their behavior so that they can benefit the most from these other efforts.

Use of these combined approaches is generally called **multimodal** therapy or intervention. Medication simply assists the individual in sitting still, paying attention, avoiding distractions, and controlling impulses. These newly acquired skills can assist learning only to the extent that educational experiences are appropriate for that person and improve behavior patterns only to the extent that expectations are defined and effort rewarded. Short-term goals of improvement in ADHD core symptoms may be partially realized by medication alone; however, maximum short-term and long-term benefits in terms of improved social adaptation and academic achievement will require a multimodal approach.

MEDICATION DECISIONS

Two questions should always be asked when considering ADHD medication for a particular individual:

Would the medication be helpful in terms of behavior regulation and
    control?
Is medication a necessary aspect of the individual's comprehensive treat-
    ment program?

These are quite different questions. Many youngsters with a profile of symptoms that could be helped by medication are adequately treated with other behavioral, educational, and/or psychological therapies. The evaluating physician has the responsibility to conclude whether medication has the potential to help a youngster. The parents and the doctor must collaborate in addressing the necessity issue, basing their decision on the severity of the youngster's symptoms and his or her response to initial behavioral, educational, and psychological efforts. Occasionally, a youngster's situation will be quite unstable; in such cases, immediate medical intervention is necessary while other treatment approaches are being developed.

The emphasis on a facilitator role for medication does not imply that medication should be postponed until all else has failed and a last-ditch effort is required. If the situation is allowed to deteriorate to this point, the youngster will be experiencing a significant loss of self-esteem. His or her interest and desire to work toward success will have disappeared. Discouragement and a sense of chronic failure will significantly reduce the possibility of positive medication benefits. Some element of self-confidence and a sense of optimism is necessary for a major improvement. In instances involving loss of self-esteem, the treatment challenge is considerably greater; disappointing results may accrue even if the medication is appropriate.

"Correct" timing in regard to medication is difficult to define. Many schools and parents tend to depend too much on medication when other modalities have not been introduced and implemented first or at the same time as medication. Medication should be considered after the response to initial environmental efforts are appreciated but before a significant deterioration in self-esteem and effort occurs. This decision is highly individualized and relates to many factors highlighted throughout this book. All participating "team" members may contribute to the process, with the final decision being made by the doctor and the parents.

Youngsters' role in understanding the need for and purpose of medication, as well as their role as partners with the medication, cannot be overemphasized. Their active role is a strong factor in determining the extent to which medications assist them in improving their behavior and performance. Emphasizing their role as active participants also allows for a sense of accomplishment and gratification when improvement occurs, as opposed to the alternative: a sense of dependency on the medication. This empowerment is extremely important when they ultimately have to take responsibility for managing their ADHD symptoms.

GENERAL PRINCIPLES OF MEDICAL INTERVENTION

- Parents should be aware of the purpose of the medication, the specific behaviors to be targeted, and potential side effects so that they have the greatest possible level of comfort entering a trial of medication. Many inquisitive parents read and ask as many questions as necessary to achieve that comfort. Most parents remain somewhat ambivalent, despite being comfortable with the decision. A successful response and the absence of significant side effects over time usually reduce hesitation and worry.

- An active communication system among parents, teachers, and physicians is essential both to acquire baseline (premedication) information regarding a youngster's behavior and to monitor the success of medical treatment. This aspect of medical therapy often is the most challenging and difficult to achieve because direct contact between physician and teacher is often cumbersome. Various questionnaires, forms, and survey instruments have been developed to assist in this process. A good evaluation should always involve completion of one of these forms, which represent the baseline observation before initiation of medication. Similar instruments are available for monitoring and observation of medication effects. If structured observations are not made, there is often confusion regarding the benefits of the medication and the best dose.

- Once the decision to use medication is made, the dosage should be adjusted for its maximum benefit. Maintaining the smallest possible dose in the name of caution is not always in a youngster's best interest. The youngster becomes exposed to all of the possible side effects without achieving the best possible benefit. Optimum doses differ and must be individualized on the basis of regular adult observations and the youngster's self-perception of her or his needs and improvement.

- Specific observable behaviors should be defined as **target behaviors** for monitoring by adults and the child. These targeted behaviors must be specific to any one youngster and may differ for different drugs being prescribed. For example, for one youngster inattention, distractibility, and task completion might be the three target behaviors for a teacher to observe when reporting the benefits of medication to the family and the prescribing doctor. Another child may need help with impulsivity, explosiveness, and social interactions.

- The dosage requirement for any given youngster may vary tremendously from the requirements for others, even those of similar age and size. The dosage requirement is often based on how efficiently youngsters metabolize the medication and excrete it from their body rather than on their size, age, or severity of symptoms. Because different drugs have different potencies, between-drug dosage comparisons are not possible.

- The prescribing doctor should indicate the side effects that might occur with any prescribed medication. Most parents prefer receiving this information in writing as well as verbally. Short- and long-term adverse effects should be discussed. It is also helpful to know which side effects are the most probable. Many parents have concerns that there are unobservable side effects that require laboratory tests or vital signs to discover. It is appropriate to inquire about side effects not mentioned by the doctor.

- The youngster's ability to determine the success of her or his own medical treatment plan is often not recognized. Many youngsters, when adequately informed and aware of target behaviors, can provide critically important information about the value of the medication and about side effects. For instance, one youngster chronically complained that a stimulant medication "slowed his brain too much while also speeding up his insides" and making him uncomfortable. Many observers, unaware of his personal concerns, felt he was much improved on the medication. His insight led to a more tolerable, equally effective medication.

- A variety of effective medications are used in treating ADHD. Parents should be aware that tolerating significant side effects in order to enjoy the benefits of medication may not be necessary. Alternative medications or various dosaging strategies can reduce, and often eliminate, side effects. For example, many youngsters do well on stimulant medications during the day but experience "rebound" at night. Such agitation and irritability is not always necessary and should not be tolerated just because school improvements have been observed. A dosing or medication change can often solve the problem.

- Most youngsters should use medication on a 7-day-a-week basis. While improvement in school functioning is usually a major goal, the youngster will probably also have difficulties at home. Parents often describe the home situation as being "manageable" without medication. However, this approach often involves excessive negative interaction with the child and can transmit the message of incompetence or unacceptability to the child by parents. If the medication is safe and tolerated for school, then certainly it is the same for weekends. Some medications must be given daily because their benefit is based on maintaining continuous blood levels. Teachers report that many youngsters who do not take medication on weekends have a more difficult time when the school week recommences.

- The long-term purpose of medication is to preserve a youngster's self-esteem. Self-esteem is often enhanced or damaged at home, by emotionally meaningful adults, as much as or more than at school. It is therefore desirable that a youngster's home behavior be appropriate so that he or she can achieve the maximum amount of encouragement and reinforcement.

- The use of medication in response to bad or inappropriate behavior should be avoided. If the medication is not used regularly on weekends, parents may respond to misbehavior or difficult situations during these off-school days by having the child take a dose of the drug. The ADHD youngster can then learn to view the medication as punishment or as the parents' means of control. Both of these perceptions lead to feelings of resistance and resentment toward the medication. Such feelings can lead to the preadolescent resisting or not complying with medication because of an unwillingness to continue to be controlled.

- Situations will arise in which extra doses of medication are desirable and approved by the doctor on an "as-needed" basis (for example, extra homework, test preparation, athletic tournaments, or stimulating social events). It is important to allow youngsters to participate in the decision about the extra dose for several reasons:

  1. It will avoid them feeling controlled by parents

  2. They will have a sense of ownership with the decision and therefore a sense of gratification when benefits accrue

  3. The process provides them experience in making life decisions regarding their ADHD that will be necessary as they get older.

- Because of the broad variety of symptoms within the profile of ADHD youngsters, combined drug therapy has become common. While it is unsettling for many parents to consider two medications when they originally were so apprehensive about even one, combined drug therapy is often the most appropriate approach. Using two drugs that address specific symptoms often allows for lower dosages of each and therefore fewer side effects. Previous approaches that involved the use of one drug in very high doses may have led to side effects that were either undesirable or may actually have accentuated the symptoms being treated. Caution is required to be certain that the two drugs are compatible. Scheduling issues must be realistic so that administering two drugs does not get too complicated. Generally, most families find it too difficult to administer drugs more than a total of three times a day.

18

Commonly Asked Questions About Medical Therapy

HOW LONG WILL MY CHILD NEED TO TAKE MEDICATION?

In the case of ADHD youngsters, this question cannot be answered. Approximately 80% of children will continue to have some symptoms into their adolescent years, but the exact number of adolescents who continue to have significant difficulties into adulthood is unknown. Many if not most adults who continue to have symptoms have learned coping strategies and made life decisions that allow for adequate functioning without medication. Others, however, can benefit considerably from medications, often the same ones used in childhood and adolescence. The challenge for most parents and professionals is to provide an environment in which the youngster can achieve as much success as possible in childhood and during the adolescent years so that he or she enters adulthood with positive self-esteem and a sense of competence.

HOW LONG WILL IT TAKE TO DETERMINE WHETHER A MEDICATION IS USEFUL AND APPROPRIATE?

The time required for a medication trial varies depending on the type of medication and the way it is absorbed and metabolized. Some medications work immediately and leave the body relatively quickly. The benefits of these drugs can be determined quite quickly, although it may take somewhat longer to establish the best dose. Other medications build up in the system, and blood levels must be established before they can provide the optimum benefit. This process often takes 3 to 4 weeks or longer. For these longer acting drugs, any change in dosage also requires a few weeks before improvement is evident.

SINCE THE DIAGNOSIS OF ADHD SEEMS TO BE A CLINICAL ONE WITH NO SPECIFIC TESTS, WHY NOT GIVE ALL YOUNGSTERS SUSPECTED OF HAVING ADHD RITALIN AND CONFIRM THE DIAGNOSIS BY THEIR RESPONSE?

This is an inappropriate way to make the diagnosis of ADHD because the youngster's apparent improvement on medication may actually be due to the positive expectations and responses of the adults in the youngster's life. When medication is given, improvement is expected. Adults begin to notice positive behavior instead of responding only to inappropriate behavior. A more positive, accepting, and reinforcing approach can often be as powerful as the medical intervention. In addition, especially for young children, improvement may occur with stimulant medication because of the artificial maturation of the child's nervous system. This maturation, in part, involves increases in neurotransmitter levels, and this is the effect of stimulant medications. Thus, a young child's immature nervous system can be temporarily matured, in an artificial manner, with medication, even if they don't have ADHD.

IS THERE AN INCREASED RISK OF SUBSTANCE ABUSE IN ADOLESCENTS WHO ARE TREATED WITH MEDICATION?

Several studies have followed children who have been appropriately diagnosed as having ADHD and treated with medication into their adolescent years. There does not appear to be any increased risk of later substance abuse. This finding may be predictable, particularly if a youngster is empowered by his or her role in the success of the medication and therefore does not become psychologically dependent on the drug. Also, appropriately treated youngsters are likely to enter their teenage years with higher self-esteem and a greater sense of success, thereby reducing their risk of substance abuse.

DO THE MEDICATIONS THAT WORK IN CHILDHOOD HAVE TO BE DISCONTINUED IN THE TEENAGE YEARS?

The medications that are useful in childhood continue to be useful in the adolescent years if the symptoms continue. Underlying biochemical differences in the nervous system, rather than age, determine the benefit of medication.

WILL SCHOOL PERSONNEL KNOW HOW TO ADMINISTER MEDICATIONS SAFELY TO ADHD YOUNGSTERS?

Public schools have a formal responsibility to administer medications (as prescribed by a physician) in a safe, consistent, and well-documented way. Schools do require an appropriately labeled prescription bottle and a note from the physician providing instructions. The resources and comfort of private schools in administering medications will vary, but most are prepared to fulfill this role. The practical aspects of a youngster's getting to the nurse's station at the right time on a daily basis must be coordinated among the classroom teacher, the nurse, and the youngster. The timing of dosages can usually be adapted somewhat to a youngster's class schedule and a nurse's availability.

DO YOUNGSTERS BECOME TOLERANT TO MEDICATIONS OVER TIME?

A few medications have a documented tolerance, with reduced clinical benefit over time, but most continue to have beneficial effects. This tolerance probably occurs because the youngster's system becomes more efficient at metabolizing and excreting the drug over time. The drug blood level is therefore reduced, as are the benefits. If a youngster's performance deteriorates, medication tolerance may be considered as the cause, along with psychological, social, and educational factors.

WILL THE DOSAGE OF THE MEDICATION HAVE TO BE INCREASED AS A YOUNGSTER GETS OLDER AND BIGGER?

The answer to this question varies tremendously from individual to individual. While many medications require an increase in dosaging because of size, ADHD youngsters are maturing as they are getting older. Frequently, this maturity can actually allow for a reduced amount of medication.

WHY DO YOUNGSTERS WHO HAVE BEEN ACCEPTING AND DOING WELL WITH MEDICATION OFTEN REJECT IT WHEN THEY REACH PREADOLESCENCE?

Because of their normal emotional development, preadolescents usually need to feel that they are like everyone else their age; if they are taking medication, they feel that they are different. In addition, they are often exerting their own independence. They may perceive the medication as a way for adults to control them, and they often reject this possibility and fight the medication. Many would also like to believe that they no longer need the medication or that it is no longer helping them. Because of their appropriate concern about their physical appearance, they often have vague fears that the medication can be harmful to them. These observations are often biased by their emotional need to not be different from their peers. It is quite common for preadolescents to reject medication; such a situation requires a sensitive, therapeutic response rather than punishment or anger.

Involving ADHD youngsters in the earliest stages of their treatment and emphasizing their role in the medication's benefits is an important part of minimizing resistance as these youngsters approach their preadolescence years. Often, a trial period in which the teenager discontinues the medication or takes a reduced dose is necessary to document the medication's value. The point can often be made to the teenager that, with the help of medication, she or he can actually function more like everyone else.

WHAT HAPPENS TO CHILDREN WHO DO NOT RESPOND TO MEDICATION?

Most children respond positively to one of the typical medications used for ADHD. For youngsters who have poor responses, combination drug therapy should be considered. The use of newer, less traditional approaches may also be necessary. Consideration should be given to additional or alternative causes of a youngster's difficulty, such as other developmental needs or emotional factors. Medication may not produce reduced benefits if it is used without adequate education or psychological support services or if the youngster is not an active treatment participant.

WHY DO SOME YOUNGSTERS TAKE MORE THAN ONE MEDICATION WHILE OTHERS SEEM FINE WITH ONLY ONE DRUG?

Youngsters who have only core symptoms (hyperactivity, inattention, distractibility, and impulsivity) can often achieve adequate treatment benefits from a single medication. Other youngsters who have a considerable number of coexisting symptoms may require two medications that specifically target their symptoms. For example, some youngsters with ADHD will have significant outbursts and exhibit negative behavioral overreactivity, explosiveness, and aggressiveness. This ADHD subtype profile often responds best to a nonstimulant medication called clonidine. Many youngsters have been given increasingly larger doses of stimulants such as Ritalin in an attempt to treat all of their symptoms. The increased dosages do not necessarily help the subtype behaviors and, in fact, may worsen them. The use of two medications, such as a stimulant and clonidine, often allows for a lower dose of both and, therefore, fewer side effects. Another common combination would be a stimulant medication and an antidepressant for ADHD youngsters with core symptoms and coexisting depression.

19

Stimulant Medications

S timulant medications are the most commonly used drugs in the treatment of ADHD. Studies have shown a 70% to 75% probability of improvement in a youngster who has been appropriately diagnosed as having ADHD and has the core symptoms of hyperactivity, inattention, distractibility, and impulsivity. Stimulant drugs probably represent the best form of medication for these core symptoms, although other medications may be useful as well.

Many parents find it confusing that a stimulant medication would actually help to calm a youngster down. A longtime myth is that stimulant medications affect ADHD youngsters in a paradoxical or reverse fashion, actually tranquilizing or calming these youngsters rather than stimulating them. This is not the case. Stimulant medications correct the presumed inadequate availability of neurotransmitters that leads to the core ADHD symptoms by increasing the availability of two neurotransmitters: norepinephrine and dopamine. This "stimulating" effect allows for more efficient processing and sorting of information, ultimately allowing youngsters to regulate their behavior and enhance their performance. The medication creates the change in neurotransmitters; the behavioral results depend on the youngster's own personal effort.

The choice of stimulant medication, along with the dose and the dosage schedule, must always be individualized. The various available stimulant medications, the dosage schedule, onset and duration of action, and advantages and disadvantages are described in Tables 2 and 3.

139

Table 2
Stimulant Medications

Medication	Form	Dosaging	Onset of action	Duration of action	Advantages/disadvantages
Ritalin (generic: methylphenidate)	Tablet 5 mg 10 mg 20 mg	Variable Generally 2–3 times per day	30–45 minutes	Variable 3–5 hours	Rapid onset of action. Predictable duration of action. Can adjust dose to needs of a given 4-hour period. Often very short duration.
Ritalin SR	Tablet 20 mg SR	Often given with regular tablet in a.m., occasionally two times per day	Variable 60–90 minutes	Variable 5–6 hours	Long acting, often avoids need for noon dose. Delayed onset, need regular tablet in a.m., may not last for school day, increase in rebound effect when wears off—tolerance noted.
Cylert (generic: pemoline)	Tablet 18.75 mg 37.5 mg 75 mg 37.5 chewable	Single daily dose in a.m.	45–60 minutes	Variable 9–14 hours Average 10 hours	Single daily dose, no stimulating effect on pulse rate or blood pressure, minimal abuse potential. Sleep problems more common. Requires baseline blood test with repeat in 4 months. Rare serious liver complications may occur.

Table 3
Stimulant Medications: The Amphetamines

Medication	Form	Dosaging	Onset of action	Duration of action	Advantages/disadvantages
Dexedrine tablets (generic: dextroamphetamine)	Tablet 5 mg	Variable Generally 2 or 3 times per day	30 minutes	Variable 3–5 hours	Approximately 1.5 to 2 times stronger than Ritalin and longer acting.
Dexedrine spansules	Capsule 5 mg 10 mg 15 mg	Alone or with tablet in a.m. Occasionally 2 times per day	45–60 minutes	Variable 6–8 hours	Longer acting, less rebound and tolerance than Ritalin SR; more likely to last school day. Several dose choices.
Adderall (generic: combination of amphetamine and dextroamphetamine)	Tablet 10 mg 20 mg	Variable 1–2 times per day	45–60 minutes	Variable 6–9 hours	Some patients feel that it lasts longer with fewer side effects, especially rebound, as compared with Dexedrine spansules. Minimal available studies to determine benefit.
Desoxyn (generic: methamphetamine)	Gradumet tablet 5 mg 10 mg 15 mg	Variable Usually once a day, may need two doses	45–60 minutes	Variable 7–8 hours	Long duration of action, possible single daily dose. High potential for abuse. Should not be used if there is a history of substance abuse.

The choice of stimulants will often depend on the prescribing doctor's experience with similar-aged youngsters with similar symptoms. Ritalin is initially prescribed more frequently than the other stimulant drugs because doctors have the most experience with it and because it has been researched more extensively. Most physicians will select a longer acting drug for children who are of junior high school age or older to avoid the necessity of taking medication at school. Most experts agree that a trial involving all three major stimulants (Ritalin, Dexedrine, and Cylert) is justified before concluding that stimulants are not useful.

General Side Effects

The potential side effects of the various stimulant medications are similar:

1. A mild to moderate decrease in appetite. Kids generally eat their usual breakfast, consumed before the medicine begins to work. Lunch intake may be decreased; by dinnertime, however, the medication effect is either gone or substantially reduced. Modifying the dosage of the drug can usually solve appetite problems.

2. Difficulty falling asleep in the evening. Stimulant medications tend to have a rather predictable duration of action. This information can be used to determine when the last dose of the day should be given.

3. Abdominal discomfort, which can be avoided if the medication is given with food. Stimulant medications should always be taken with food to enhance their absorption into the system.

4. Headaches, particularly if the child has had a previous history of vascular or migraine-type headaches. These headaches tend to occur when the effects of the medication wear off.

5. Moodiness or weepiness. During the first week of medication use, children may feel slightly moody or weepy in the afternoon when the effects of the drug wear off. This effect will disappear after that time period as their system becomes accustomed to the stimulating effect.

6. Mild increase in heart rate and blood pressure. This change (usually about a 5% increase) is of no clinical concern and will not affect the child's health or ability to exercise.

7. Rebound. A very small number of children experience rebound, which occurs when the medication wears off. The youngster may become more hyperactive and irritable, even though the medication was quite helpful

during the day. This side effect seems to occur in youngsters who metabolize the drug in a manner such that it leaves their system abruptly. Dosing adjustments often resolve the problem.

8. Irritability. A few children become irritable, tense, and agitated with stimulant medication. A low test dose for the first day or two is often a good idea so that this side effect will be relatively mild and last only a few hours. This type of response may indicate that stimulants are not an appropriate medication choice for that youngster.

SPECIFIC SIDE EFFECTS

Ritalin and Tourette's Syndrome

There have been some concerns regarding Ritalin and its association with Tourette's syndrome. It is quite clear at this point that Ritalin *does not* cause Tourette's syndrome. Tourette's syndrome is a chronic neurological condition involving motor and vocal tics, obsessive-compulsive behavior, extreme behavioral outbursts, and various repetitive habit-like gestures. Approximately 65% of individuals with Tourette's will have symptoms of an attentional disorder that is identical to and indistinguishable from ADHD. Often, these attention symptoms occur before the tics develop. If a youngster has Tourette's syndrome and has the associated attentional problems but no tics, taking a stimulant medication may bring on the tics earlier in life than otherwise would have been the case. The medication did not cause the Tourette's but allowed the symptoms to emerge earlier than they might have. Most of the research surrounding this phenomenon has involved Ritalin. The relative risks occurring with the other stimulant medications are probably comparable, although this has not been firmly documented.

If the preceding scenario occurs and the stimulant medication is discontinued, the tics often decline in intensity, but there is no guarantee that they will totally disappear. No physician can absolutely predict whether this scenario will occur in any given child. However, the relative risk can often be estimated via the coexistence of tic or Tourette's symptoms and a family history of tic disorder symptoms or other suspicious symptoms.

Cylert and the Liver

There have also been concerns regarding the effect of Cylert on the liver. Recent evidence indicates that only about 0.3% to 0.5% of individuals taking Cylert may have an apparent inflammation of their liver, along with increased levels of liver enzymes in their bloodstream (as identified through blood tests). (Previous statistics had indicated that this complication occurs in 2% of patients.) This possible effect on the liver has always been shown to be reversible when the medication is discontinued.

If a youngster is prescribed Cylert, a baseline determination of her or his liver function is necessary, and this procedure should probably be repeated every 4 months. The manufacturer of the drug has recently reported a very rare complication of acute liver failure that occurred 13 times from 1975 to 1996. This severe, and at times fatal, complication occurred during a period in which 7.2 million prescriptions for Cylert were written. In all of the cases, the individual had been taking Cylert for at least 6 months. Routine blood tests may not identify such patients.

Stimulant Medications and Growth

Finally, concerns have arisen regarding the effect of stimulant medications, especially Ritalin, on growth. Long-term studies of young adults who have taken stimulant medications indicate that their growth is identical to that of their siblings, regardless of how long they have been on stimulant medications. Short-term studies show that a very small percentage of youngsters who take Ritalin do evidence a slowdown in their growth velocity. If these youngsters are identified through regular monitoring and taken off the medication for two consecutive summers, there is no apparent long-term effect on their growth. Another study indicated a catch-up growth during adolescence resulting in expected adult height. With proper monitoring and treatment responses, there should be no concern regarding stimulant medications and long-term growth.

DOSE DETERMINATION

The specific dose of a stimulant medication is determined by a number of factors and must be individualized.

- The initial dosage should be determined through a carefully monitored process involving as little expectation bias as possible. For example, one approach to initiating stimulant medications is for the teacher to remain unaware of the dosage given to the child on any given day. Teachers should be made aware that the child is receiving medication but not be made aware of the doses given on any given day over a

2-week period of time. On the various days the dose is randomized from a low dose to a typically optimal dose for that child. On some days during the 2-week period, the child receives no medication. The teacher is then asked to comment on three specific target behaviors for each day. After the 2-week period, the correlation is made between the dosage for a particular day and the teacher's comments. This system will allow the opportunity to determine whether the medication effect is noticeably different than no medication at all and, it is hoped, the ability to determine the lowest best dose for initial treatment. Once the initial dose is established, careful monitoring in terms of clinical benefits is necessary. The need for modifying the dose may occur unexpectedly based on factors such as a change in school schedule, a change in home schedule, the style and approach of different teachers, stress factors, and the demand for a youngster's attention during his or her typical daily activities.

- Medication is considered to be a facilitator for environmental efforts only; however, once the decision to use medication is made, the substance should be used to provide optimal functioning for the youngster for as many of her or his waking hours as possible. Many clinicians and parents presume that the primary purpose of medication is to improve school functioning. While this indeed is an important issue, the goal of therapy is to enhance the youngster's overall functioning. Thus, once it is determined that the medication is valuable, the dose should be determined in a way that enhances the youngster's functioning at school, during activities, with peers, and at home. This principle is intended not to justify large doses of medication to achieve "the perfect child" but to allow the child success in as many areas as possible. Daylong success for children with ADHD is imperative both to enhance their self-esteem and to balance the areas of weakness in their lives.

- The duration of action for stimulant medications varies enormously among individuals. For example, the effects of short-acting Ritalin and Dexedrine typically last 3 to 5 hours. The range, however, may be anywhere from 1.5 to 6 or 7 hours. Typically, for each of the stimulant medications, the duration of action is well defined. If a youngster takes Ritalin tablets and the clinical effects persist for 4 hours and 20 minutes, it is likely that the duration of action will be predictably the same every time the medication is administered. This characteristic of stimulant medications makes it fairly easy to determine the best interval for administration.

- Duration of action is not typically changed to any significant degree by the amount of medication. Efforts to prolong the duration of action usually require an additional dose or a change in scheduling, not simply an increase in the amount of the original dose.

- While youngsters' size, height, and weight are relevant to the appropriate dose, these characteristics are not the sole determining factors. Individuals' metabolic rate determines how rapidly the medication is used and excreted from their body. This fact highlights the necessity of individualizing doses. For example, a 5-year-old may require 20 milligrams per dose of Ritalin, whereas a 20-year-old may require 5 milligrams. This fact also emphasizes the need to individualize the initial trial period to allow determination of the lowest dose for any child.

- For most pediatric medications, a larger dose is required as a youngster gets older. In the case of stimulant medication, the dosage requirement may actually decrease with age because of the enhanced maturity of the youngster's nervous system and his or her improved inherent ability in terms of behavior regulation. Successful learned coping strategies may also reduce the need for medication.

- In the past, it was believed that stimulant medications were appropriate only for children and adolescents. Research now indicates that older adolescents, young adults, and even older adults can benefit from stimulant medications, probably because their underlying neurotransmitter variations are the same as those of children.

- A monitoring system involving feedback from the youngster, the parents, and teachers must be established prior to initiating a trial of medication. While the initial trial period typically involves intense observation, a long-term monitoring mechanism is equally important.

- Global feedback should be avoided. Monitoring should always be specific to target symptoms and time of day. For example, parents and teachers often complain that the medication is no longer valuable, often leading to a change in the overall daily medication dose. However, typically the youngster is having difficulty at one specific point in time through the school day or at home that involves the duration of action of the medication or the inadequacy of one of the multiple daily dosages. Concerns about the medication's benefits should therefore be addressed by answering questions such as the following:

  Exactly when and where is the youngster having the greatest difficulty? When does the medication seem to be working effectively?

Could the behavior of concern be a withdrawal or rebound effect from the medication rather than a lack of clinical benefit?

Is the difficult behavior actually medication related, or could a change in structure, definition of expectations, or other factors be more relevant?

These and other probing questions must be answered, particularly when a youngster who has previously been doing well begins to have difficulty.

- Avoid tunnel vision regarding a youngster's functioning. Many parents and teachers are so intent on improving target behaviors that they fail to recognize the adverse effects of the medication, which create their own sets of problems. For example, many youngsters will complain about tiredness on stimulant medication, which is typically an effect of too much medication or overdosing. Because the child may be less hyperactive, less fidgety, and somewhat more attentive in the classroom, his or her complaints are either ignored or recognized without a helpful response. The net result may be that the youngster has less of a behavior problem but in fact is less productive because of the fatigue factor is therefore not benefiting from the medication for long-term goals as intended. Another example is the use of stimulant medications that cause insomnia and make it difficult for the child to fall asleep. This side effect is tolerated because of the marked improvement in daily activities with the medication. Unfortunately, the youngster is chronically fatigued as a result of falling asleep 2 or 3 hours later than usual and is not meeting personal requirements for sleep.

  Some youngsters will experience rebound with stimulant medications. They benefit tremendously from the medication during its clinical activity but become irritable, agitated, or hyperactive beyond their nonmedicated state when the medication wears off. This withdrawal effect is often tolerated because of the benefits of the medication, despite the fact that the youngster is in conflict with everyone around her or him during this period. Therefore, while enjoying the specific benefits of medication, careful sight must be maintained on the youngster's overall functioning, and close attention must be paid to detrimental side effects that actually may sabotage the entire therapeutic effort.

- Stimulant medications has been the primary treatment for ADHD. This general principle remains appropriate. However, frequently, doses of stimulant medications are gradually increased to an extremely high level to treat resistant symptoms that would best be treated by an alternative medication. A clinical history will make the point. A 7-year-old boy with ADHD moved to a new community. The new physician discovered that he was on 120 milligrams of Ritalin per day. In his previous community he had a pediatrician, a psychologist, and a psychiatrist. Complaints of inadequate medication benefit to all three of these professionals led to a gradual increase in dosages. He was sleeping poorly, losing weight because of his loss of appetite, and generally continued to have behavioral difficulty. His medication was gradually totally withdrawn. The new physician discovered that he was behaviorally the same on no medication as he had been on 120 milligrams of Ritalin per day. The target behavior that previous clinicians were attempting to treat was explosive outbursts with severe behavioral negative overreactivity, which apparently was not amenable to and did not benefit from Ritalin. It would have been wiser to either attempt a trial with another stimulant or move on to a different class of medication when this clinical reality became apparent. Instead, the dose was increased on numerous occasions, only to bring on more and more undesirable and intolerable side effects.

- Some controversy exists regarding the use of stimulant medications on weekends, during extended holiday vacations, and during the summer. The use of medication 7 days a week is highly desirable because of the benefits of optimal functioning rather than "manageability" for youngsters at home on weekends. The need for medication on extended holidays also exists. The pace of life is often increased, structure is decreased, defined expectations are somewhat inconsistent, and the level of stimulation is enhanced. For these reasons, life can become more difficult for a youngster with ADHD and reduce his or her ability to be in control, thus reducing the enjoyment of the holiday activities for everyone. Continued use of medication for these time periods is therefore recommended. Many youngsters have busy summers full of both scheduled and unscheduled activities. Success during these activities is just as relevant to a youngster's overall self-esteem as school performance. Medication should therefore be made available during those time periods.

A summer drug holiday of 2 to 3 weeks is recommended for most children on stimulant medication. The purpose of this drug holiday is to observe the youngster's baseline behavior without medication in comparison to the premedicated state or the observations made during the previous summer. This drug holiday period allows for a modification of the stimulant medication dosage depending upon the perception of the youngster's needs. Many youngsters who have an improved baseline ability without the medication can have a reduction in their dosage or, at some point in time, a trial of no medication as the school year begins. These drug holidays are typically recommended during the latter part of the summer when activities are over, and prior to the beginning of school.

- The potential for side effects of stimulant medications often lasts beyond the observed clinical benefit. For example, the youngster's beneficial response to stimulant medication, as measured by ability to pay attention and avoid distractions, may have worn off, while lack of appetite or inability to fall asleep may persist for several hours beyond that time. This observation is not true for all youngsters on stimulant medications but may be relevant for some.

- As mentioned earlier, because of clinical improvements, some clinicians, teachers, and parents will desire continued use of the medication at a specific dose, regardless of observed side effects. This decision may be tolerable for some period of time since some adverse effects will diminish as the youngster remains on the medication. For example, some youngsters become slightly irritable in the first week of two of medical therapy when the medication wears off. This side effect generally disappears if it is mild to begin with. Rebound may also improve somewhat but may also worsen over time. Appetite-suppressing effects, if significant, typically remain but may gradually improve to the point of acceptability. A major adverse effect such as becoming irritable and agitated at the earliest stages of a trial is not likely to get better with time. Difficulty falling asleep may improve somewhat with time as the youngster becomes more experienced with the medication and metabolizes it more efficiently. Therefore, for many adverse effects a brief observation period to determine improvement is justified, particularly if the medication is very helpful. However, intolerable side effects cannot be justified in the name of trying to help a youngster.

TRICKS OF THE TRADE

Various strategies have been discovered to improve specific behavioral difficulties or allow adverse effects to be more acceptable.

- Early morning behavioral regulation is typically difficult for many youngsters with ADHD. All family members become stressed by the requirements of awakening at a reasonable time and preparing for school and work. Generally, stimulant medications take approximately

30 to 45 minutes to begin working, with the onset of improvement occurring just as a youngster walks out the door after a tumultuous, unsettling start of the day. Many youngsters can benefit by receiving a stimulant medication 30 to 60 minutes before awakening. The youngster simply is asked to sit up and swallow a pill, then return to sleep until wakeup time. With this strategy, the youngster is often more able to meet the demands of preparing for school. The youngster can then be given his or her usual morning dose for the day, as usually prescribed with breakfast. This strategy is not solely intended to make life easier for parents. A youngster who has had a smooth early morning period generally arrives at school calmer, less unsettled, and more prepared to deal with the demands of the school setting.

- Long-acting stimulants may have a longer onset of action than short-acting stimulants. This is not universally true, with many youngsters showing clinical improvement within 30 to 45 minutes. For youngsters in whom there is a delay, a long-acting medication can be combined with a short-acting medication for the morning dose. The short-acting medication allows for a relatively rapid improvement before the long-acting medication begins working.

- Combining various stimulant medications is acceptable since they work so similarly. For example, a Dexedrine spansule might assist a middle school youngster through the entire school day but may wear off before evening homework time. Since short-acting Dexedrine may last too long and affect sleep, short-acting Ritalin, which typically is not quite as long acting as Dexedrine, can be given after school. The Ritalin may well wear off before bedtime and allow the youngster to sleep effectively. The onset of action of Cylert, which comes only in a long-acting form, in some youngsters may be delayed. Ritalin or Dexedrine can be given with the Cylert to solve this problem.

- A youngster's usual dose of medication may not allow optimal functioning for specific events such as athletic events, competitive tournaments, or performances. The decision to use additional medications for these experiences is reasonable. The decision should always be made in collaboration with the child based on his or her perception of the demands of that situation and desire to effectively enhance functioning. It is quite important to avoid parents' desire for achievement as the sole deciding factor in this decision because of the additional stress experienced by a child under these circumstances. He or she may also become resentful of the parents' taking over and deciding what's best.

■ For youngsters who have intolerable appetite suppression with stimulant medications, various strategies are possible. Second or school doses of medication may be given after lunch so that the youngster's appetite is not excessively suppressed. One caution regarding this approach: If the morning dose has already worn off, allowing the youngster to eat, behavior may be far less than desirable during the lunch break recess because of the lack of medical benefit at that point in time. While this strategy may allow a larger lunch, the behavioral consequences may not justify it. The dose of stimulant medication may be reduced on weekends for youngsters with extreme appetite suppression, especially if associated with considerable weight loss. Multivitamins with minerals should also be given. Some parents have found that the ingestion of a 6-ounce can of high-protein drink on a daily basis can compensate for the lack of food intake at meals.

■ Rarely, some youngsters will actually sleep better with a stimulant medication in their system, as compared with the typical insomnia effect of stimulants. These youngsters may be able to lay in bed in a quiet room and tolerate the continuous subtle stimulation with the help of medication rather than feel bombarded by their perception of this stimulation, which precludes their sleep. Some parents discover this phenomenon when medication is either purposefully or inadvertently administered later in the day and remains in a youngster's system at bedtime. A caution regarding this idea: The medication should not be given at bedtime based on this possibility because of the consequences of insomnia and the youngster being awake for an entire night. Administering an afternoon dose slightly later might be a way to test the possibility if there is clinical suspicion of this benefit.

20

Other Medical Therapies

Since people with ADHD are more different than they are alike, it is not surprising that different medications might be necessary for different individuals. Initial medication treatment efforts may lead to disappointing results or to intolerable side effects. Alternative medications must then be sought. Because of increases in the diagnosis of ADHD and because of the lack of responsiveness by some youngsters to the medications commonly used, many alternative medications have been tried clinically and in research settings.

It is important not to discount or refuse to use a medication simply because of its drug classification. For example, many parents object to the use of antidepressants to treat their ADHD youngster. Quite often, these medications are used not because of their antidepressant qualities but because they work in a manner similar to that of stimulant medications but without the stimulating side effects. The prescribing doctor is more interested in the biological or neurotransmitter effect of the medication than in its drug classification. Parents need to learn the facts about each proposed medication, ask all possible questions, and then gain a personal level of comfort before proceeding.

Medication can be valuable in two ways. First, it can produce a clinical benefit for the youngster. Second, the use of various medications provides the only window of opportunity for the doctor to understand the biochemical variations for a particular individual. As discussed earlier, none of the underlying biochemical mechanisms presumed to cause ADHD have been definitively proven. There is, however, strong evidence regarding the variations that typically occur when certain symptoms are present. The use of various medications can clarify, to some extent, biological variations. For example, if several stimulant medications are used and the youngster becomes more hyperactive, irritable, and agitated, then the common underlying biochemical variation presumed for most ADHD youngsters probably *is not* the variation for that particular child. Alternative drugs can then be chosen.

Occasionally, youngsters with very complicated symptoms have previously undergone trials of multiple medications. A careful review of the benefits and side effects of each medication can provide a great deal of insight to the prescribing physician regarding remaining medical options.

All of the medications described in this chapter have potential benefits in terms of management of ADHD and coexisting symptoms. The specific target behaviors being treated should be carefully defined before initiation of use. Questions regarding side effects should be answered, and monitoring programs should be in place. The various commonly used medications are discussed, along with the indications for their use and possible side effects.

TRICYCLIC ANTIDEPRESSANTS

Indications

Several tricyclic antidepressant drugs have been used successfully in the treatment of ADHD:

Imipramine (Tofranil)
Desipramine (Norpramin)
Amitriptyline (Elavil)
Nortriptyline (Pamelor or Aventil)
Clomipramine (Anafranil)

These drugs may be indicated in situations in which (a) stimulant drugs are not tolerated (for example, because of the severity of their side effects), (b) stimulant drugs are ineffective or inadequately effective, (c) there is a significant amount of depression or anxiety associated with the ADHD symptoms, or (d) motor tics occur in association with core ADHD symptoms. Also, they may be used in combination with stimulants to accentuate and sustain the latter's clinical benefits.

These medications are similar to stimulants in terms of biochemical or neurotransmitter benefit, but they have fewer stimulating side effects. Because of their long-acting nature, they require established blood levels. Each dose is intended to maintain the blood level rather than having an immediate clinical benefit. Adults may take these medications only once a day. Because children and adolescents metabolize drugs more efficiently, they generally require two or three doses a day to sustain effective blood levels. The long-acting nature of these medications allows for 24-hour-a-day benefits but requires regular administration for sustained improvement. A partial improvement may be seen a few days after use has been initiated, but full effects often require 2 to 3 weeks. Lower doses are generally helpful for core ADHD symptoms, while higher doses may be required to improve depressive symptoms and mood swings.

Side Effects

Antidepressant medications may be sedating or cause fatigue for children and adolescents. This side effect can often be minimized by administration of larger doses in the evening than during the day. Tricyclic antidepressants generally slow down the intestinal tract and may cause dry mouth or constipation. The medication should be used cautiously with youngsters who have preexisting difficulties with chronic constipation. The constipation may require the use of stool softeners or adjustments in diet by increasing fluids and fiber.

Tricyclic antidepressants can affect the electrical signal in the heart muscle, causing a change in heartbeat and heart rhythm. For this reason, a baseline electrocardiogram is necessary before use of the medication is initiated. Most often, the EKG (electrocardiogram) is normal, allowing full use of the medication. Occasionally the results will be borderline, requiring repeat of the electrocardiogram a few weeks after drug initiation. In a few rare instances, the baseline EKG findings do not allow the use of these medications. The necessity to repeat the EKG will depend on the baseline results and the ultimate dosage of the medication.

The physiologic effects of tricyclics must be monitored. Heart rate typically is increased but must be maintained within a safe level. The level of medication in the blood can be measured via a blood test. This measurement may not be necessary in all cases, but it can be useful in determining whether larger doses can be given or whether the youngster is experiencing toxic or overdose effects from too much medication.

Missing a dose or two of medication is not dangerous; however, temporary symptoms of headache, stomachache, nausea, and aching muscles may occur. Some children may show signs of nervousness, sadness, or difficulty sleeping. A significant tricyclic overdose can be quite dangerous, causing seizures and serious cardiac effects. It is particularly important to control access to these medications. They should be kept out of the reach of young children. The intake of youngsters of all ages should be monitored carefully.

ANTIHYPERTENSIVE AGENTS

Indications

Two medications in this category have become popular in the treatment of ADHD: clonidine (Catapres) and guanfacine (Tenex).

These medications have been used primarily in adults to treat high blood pressure. They have recently been used for children and adolescents with ADHD, particularly those who have coexisting symptoms of:

- Significant behavioral negative overreactivity

- Major behavioral outbursts

- Oppositional defiant behavior

- Major impulsivity

- Aggression

- Tic disorder or Tourette's syndrome

These medications may not be quite as effective as stimulant medications in terms of improving attention levels and reducing distractibility; thus, they are often used in combination with stimulant medications. Prior to the availability of these medications, large doses of stimulants were often used to treat a broad range of symptoms, including some of those just listed. It is now believed that combination therapy may allow for use of relatively smaller doses of these medicines, resulting in better clinical benefits and fewer side effects.

Because they are long acting, antihypertensive agents require the establishment and maintenance of a drug blood level in order to be effective. Clonidine typically requires dosing three times a day, while guanfacine can often be used twice a day. Clonidine is available in a skin patch called Catapres-TTS that was developed for individuals with high blood pressure. Use in ADHD individuals may be helpful in terms of establishing sustained, even blood levels without concern about multiple daily dosages. However, skin rashes occur rather frequently despite rotation of the site of the patch.

When the patch is successfully tolerated, it generally is helpful for only 4 to 5 days rather than an entire week; as a result, more frequent replacement is required.

Side Effects

Most individuals who take clonidine or guanfacine have initial sedation or fatigue that improves as the drug is continued. For this reason, the drug should be gradually introduced, the dose being built up slowly based on the amount of fatigue. Occasionally an adequate, effective dose cannot be achieved because of persistent excessive fatigue. Guanfacine is less sedating and can be used when intolerable fatigue occurs with clonidine. Generally, in children and adolescents, blood pressure is minimally affected by these agents unless high blood pressure was present prior to initiation of use. Headaches and dizziness may be noted in the first few weeks; these symptoms improve with time. Sleep can occasionally be disrupted, and appetite may be increased. Increases and decreases in weight have been observed. The medication cannot be stopped abruptly because of withdrawal effects that may include rapid heartbeat, high blood pressure, agitation, anxiousness, headaches, and stomachaches. The medication can be safely discontinued in a gradual manner.

OTHER ANTIDEPRESSANTS

Bupropion (Wellbutrin)

Indications

Bupropion has been studied in individuals with attention disorders who may or may not have coexisting depression. The medication has been shown to be effective but probably should be reserved for (a) individuals with ADHD who have not tolerated or benefitted from stimulant medications, (b) instances in which significant depression coexists with attention disorder symptoms, and (c) instances in which ADHD and depression have not responded adequately to other medications. Bupropion works by establishing blood levels and usually requires dosing twice or three times a day. A sustain release has recently become available. The biochemical effects are not certain but may be similar to those of stimulant medications and tricyclic antidepressants.

Side Effects

Reported side effects include agitation, insomnia, headache, nausea, vomiting, and constipation. In general, bupropion is reasonably well tolerated. There are concerns regarding seizures or convulsions, which have been seen in about 4 of 1,000 (0.4%) individuals treated with this medication.

Selective Serotonin Reuptake Inhibitor Antidepressants

Indications

The medications in this category are:

Fluoxetine (Prozac)
Sertraline (Zoloft)
Paroxetine (Paxil)
Fluvoxamine (Luvox)

The biologic effect of these agents is to increase the availability of serotonin between brain cells, in much the same manner that stimulants and tricyclic antidepressants increase levels of dopamine and norepinephrine. These drugs may be indicated for depression, anxiety disorders, and obsessive-compulsive disorders, all of which coexist with ADHD. Because of the benefits of fluoxetine shown in some adults, the drugs have been used in ADHD adolescents who are not responsive to stimulants but who are not necessarily depressed. Some studies have indicated significant improvement in these teenagers, while others have shown disappointing results. There is a documented benefit for ADHD individuals who have coexisting depression when these drugs are used in combination with stimulants. In general, reuptake inhibitors have been shown to be more effective than tricyclic antidepressants in treating childhood and adolescent depression.

Side Effects

Side effects can include agitation, sleeplessness, gastrointestinal symptoms of nausea, constipation, and diarrhea. These medications are generally well tolerated. Low doses of one of these agents, in combination with a stimulant, can be quite effective in the management of individuals with ADHD who also evidence anxiety or depression.

OTHER MEDICATIONS

A variety of other medications have been used in individuals with ADHD, including thioridazine (Mellaril), haloperidol (Haldol), lithium (Eskalith), carbamazepine (Tegretol), valproic acid (Depakote), and, more recently, venlafaxine (Effexor) and risperidone (Risperidone). These drugs are generally necessary only in individuals with ADHD who have more severe psychiatric and behavioral disturbances and for those who have not benefitted from the more traditional medications discussed earlier. They all have greater probable benefit for different profiles of symptoms and possible short- and long-term side effects. As with any medication, parents should review all available information in order to achieve a level of comfort before proceeding.

21

Nontraditional ADHD Therapies

B ecause of the frequent occurrence of ADHD and because of many parents' inherent discomfort with medication, alternative treatment approaches have been sought from a variety of professionals. These nontraditional therapies can be defined as those that are not well researched and do not have a scientific basis that would predict benefit in a majority of situations. They are often promoted and heralded by lay individuals and professionals with evangelistic beliefs about potential benefits.

DIETARY MANAGEMENT

Dietary management, perhaps the most commonly used alternative intervention, has revolved around sugar, food additives, and food colorings; the use of vitamin and mineral supplements; and food allergies. The limited dietary research that has been done is often difficult to interpret. Many of the subjects were receiving other treatments at the time of the study. Also, this type of research (as is true with some of the medication studies) is heavily biased by the expectation of improvement. When parents make a major change in their child's diet, they generally are more sensitive and pay greater attention to the child's behavior, especially positive and appropriate behaviors. Prior to the diet, only negative behaviors may have been noticed. Often, the presumption is that the "improvement" is due to the change in diet. Noting the positive behavior by rewarding or complimenting the child inherently increases the motivation of the child to behave better. The continued improvement is typically attributed to the diet change, when in fact it may be due more to the behavior reinforcement. The diet change is continued and acclaimed because of its apparent improvement. Unfortunately, this conclusion eventually leads to a reduction in behavioral reinforcement and a regression in terms of appropriate behavior because the diet had nothing to do with the improvement in the first place.

Refined Sugar

While sugar, specifically refined sugar, appears to worsen the behavior of many children with ADHD, there is no scientific proof that this occurs. Advocates who believe that excessive sugar causes behavioral and attentional problems have focused on the occurrence of temporary hypoglycemia, or low blood sugar. This has not been documented in numerous studies. In fact, all studies that have been done have failed to demonstrate a correlation between sugar intake and behavior.

While sugar probably does not cause an attention disorder, it may result in stress to ADHD individuals' vulnerable nervous systems, in addition to neurotransmitter variations. There is no laboratory test to document this possibility. Withholding sugar is the only reasonable diagnostic test. A sugar-free diet should be attempted to determine whether an ADHD child or adolescent is, in fact, sugar-sensitive. If improved behavior regulation is noted, attempts should be made to continue with the reduced sugar intake. Other medical considerations, such as obesity, dental health, and the relative lack of nutritional value of sugar, support controlled sugar intake for all children and adolescents.

Food Allergies

Food allergies have not been clearly defined as a cause of behavioral disturbances in children. They may be suspected clinically and through traditionally available allergy tests, but such tests do not necessarily determine the impact of allergies on a youngster's behavior. If the youngster suffers extensive respiratory, intestinal, or skin manifestations of a food allergy, the suspected food should be withdrawn to improve these clinical symptoms. Some behavioral improvement may be noted under these circumstances, but this treatment should not be relied upon as a predictably effective treatment for ADHD, especially in lieu of more traditional approaches. Foods that have been most highly implicated are milk, wheat, eggs, and corn.

Food Colorings and Food Additives

Dr. Benjamin Feingold, an allergist, popularized the idea that the salicylate structures of many food colorings and food additives are causes of hyperactivity and other behavioral disturbances. While his view was enormously popular when it was first proposed, there has been little scientific evidence to support this approach. Scientific studies have shown that perhaps one half of 1% of all ADHD youngsters are sensitive to these substances, but no studies have defined which youngsters are most likely to be affected. If parents choose to test the benefit of this approach, yellow tartrazine and red dye number 2 have been the substances most implicated. It is recommended that traditional treatments be continued during these trials.

Megavitamins and Mineral Substances

Megavitamins and mineral substances have also been proposed as treatments for ADHD. There has been no proof that a deficiency in terms of these vitamins in an otherwise healthy child or adolescent causes behavioral problems. Furthermore, there is no evidence supporting these interventions as being successful. In fact, excessive doses of vitamins can actually be harmful; for example, excessive intake of Vitamin C may cause kidney stones.

NEUROTHERAPY

Neurotherapy with EEG biofeedback has recently gained popularity. This approach developed because of observations, from EEG and brain wave studies, that individuals with ADHD mobilize slow brain waves when they attempt to concentrate, as opposed to the necessary rapid brain waves. A diagnostic test is available to discern whether this phenomenon is present in a given individual. Through biofeedback, the individual can be taught, via a computer model, to increase his or her fast waves as demanded in learning and concentration situations. While a great deal of enthusiasm exists for this approach, controlled studies are lacking. There is also concern that office-based skills don't generalize to the classroom or to home life. Furthermore, this treatment rarely occurs without the youngster receiving other therapies, making the interpretation of studies difficult. Such an approach requires substantial resources in terms of time and money. Often, 30 to 40 sessions are required, and these sessions are most effective if they take place over a relatively brief period of time. As a result, this approach is expensive. Enthusiasm for the approach might increase with an increased number of controlled studies and documentation of benefits.

ANTI-MOTION SICKNESS MEDICATIONS

Anti-motion sickness medications are advocated by professionals who believe that there is a relationship between ADHD and problems with coordination and balance. These individuals believe that inner ear dysfunctions in regard to control of balance are a cause of ADHD, particularly in terms of difficulty in movement regulation. There is, at the present time, no evidence to support the use of these medications by themselves or in conjunction with stimulant medications.

VISION TRAINING

Vision or optometric training has been advocated by developmental optometrists who believe that reading problems are caused by faulty eye movements. Visual training has been advocated to treat both reading problems and attention disorders. A small number of individuals with reading problems may have apparent eye-motor coordination difficulties as the source of their reading problems, and they may benefit from this therapy. However, there is no evidence that these such exercises promote behavioral regulation and control in children or adolescents.

NEUROSENSORY INTEGRATION DYSFUNCTION THERAPY

Neurosensory integration dysfunction therapy falls under the field of occupational therapy. The symptoms of this dysfunction are described in Chapter 3. As mentioned, these symptoms are believed to result from a dysfunction in the balance control system in the inner ear. Therapies involve a variety of strategies, including rolling a youngster on a large therapy ball, rotational swinging, and brushing the skin, as well as techniques to improve fine and gross motor coordination. Most physicians reject the value of this approach because they do not believe that moving the body or brushing the skin can change the nervous system and allow the child to better tolerate stimulation, thus resulting in improved behavioral regulation. It is understandable that brushing the skin can have a calming effect on a child who is out of control. Preparing the nervous system for future experiences is another matter. However, while there is not a full understanding of how these therapies work, significant and, at times, dramatic benefits have been observed.

If a youngster has several of the ADHD symptoms described in this book, an evaluation by a qualified, experienced occupational therapist is quite reasonable. If the results confirm the diagnosis, the intervention should be considered on a time-limited basis. Most therapists will encourage that educational, behavioral, and medical treatments be continued during this effort.

SUMMARY

Many inquisitive parents will read about treatment approaches not yet recommended by any professional on their youngster's treatment team. These approaches are often presented with great enthusiasm and with multiple testimonials from parents. Parents should investigate such treatments to the extent possible and then bring the information to the attention of the most appropriate involved professional for an opinion. Several questions should be addressed:

1. Is the treatment relevant to the youngster's symptoms and profile?

2. Is there a reasonable chance of benefit?

3. Can the approach be detrimental or harmful?

4. Should an additional professional be sought who might have greater knowledge of and experience with the treatment?

5. If the treatment is pursued, should the existing "traditional" approaches be modified in any way?

If parents perceive that their interest in any treatment has not been given reasonable, reflective attention, they should seek an additional professional response.

22

Getting Started: Organizing Your Efforts

You, as parents, will always be the primary advocates for your child's ADHD and will always represent the continuity in his or her care. While many professionals may be involved, their perspective will be limited to the relatively brief time frame in which they have known your child. Your historical perspective is critical to provide guidance to those professionals and to ensure that successful treatments are continued and unsuccessful ones are not repeated. Many parents have commented that they feel like they must be therapists for their child with ADHD during every waking moment of every day. Fortunately or unfortunately, this statement represents the truth. Generally, prior to an appropriate evaluation and the development of a treatment program, most parents spend a great deal of time in an uncoordinated, often chaotic fashion without producing the desired results or outcome. After a meaningful evaluation, the first step is for you, as parents, to become as educated regarding ADHD as possible. Then start your intervention effort, which will allow your expenditure of energy to be more organized, specific to your child's needs, and, thus, more productive.

Over time, most parents find it difficult to remember all of the facts they've learned, to keep track of all of the evaluations that have occurred, and to recall the outcomes of various treatments. This chapter is devoted to helping you maintain an effective level of organization as you begin and continue the treatment program for your child. While the use of the proposed forms may seem cumbersome, this information, in the long run, will be extremely valuable. After several years of active treatment for their children, many parents find themselves with folder after folder and box after box of materials.

Suggestions for getting organized are divided into five sections here and match the forms in the Appendix. The forms are intended to help you keep track of all relevant information and to highlight experiences in a summary fashion for better long-term recall. Maintaining these forms will also allow your youngster to have a full sense of his or her evaluation and treatment history as he or she becomes more independent and takes control over treatment. The suggestions provided here will not be appropriate for all families. Read them carefully, consider each one, and use the ones that appear to be the most relevant for your child and your family.

PARENTAL SELF-EDUCATION

- Self-education is essential to understanding your ADHD child's or adolescent's needs. A variety of reading materials, audiotapes, and videotapes are available that provide factual information for parents and youngsters of all ages. The resource section of this book contains a list of such materials. Most books regarding ADHD include important information and reasonable recommendations. These books should be read as a class curriculum rather than casually. As you read, you will gain a sense of whether the information is relevant to your child and whether the recommendations are appropriate to his or her needs. Keep notes as you read for best recall.

- As you begin your self-education process and the intervention program for your ADHD youngster, it is helpful to keep a running list of questions that arise on a day-to-day basis. As questions are answered, they can be crossed out and eliminated. This approach allows you to focus your learning and also to have a list of important questions available when you read or when you meet with the various professionals involved with your child.

- As you review books, videotapes, and audiotapes, you might find it useful to briefly highlight, in note form, the most important major information you have learned during any particular reading or listening period. These notes can be periodically reviewed as one would review in preparation for a final examination. This approach will keep your information current and lead to new questions for future reading.

EVALUATION RECORD

▪ A diary of evaluations is useful to keep in a record form. It is also useful to keep notes, in your own words, of the evaluator's conclusions. These records can be very useful when recalling the history for another assessment. Also, noting the exact location of previous evaluations can allow for rapid retrieval of reports when they are lost or misplaced.

GOAL SETTING

▪ The management of ADHD involves both short- and long-term goals. Short-term goal setting is important for you and your youngster because it will allow for a focus of your energies. Goals are set in regard to a sense of priorities providing specific direction. It is suggested that you set short-term goals for approximately 3 to 4 months at a time. One goal each in the area of personal/social development, family interactions, academics, and therapeutic intervention should be set and monitored. At the end of this 3- to 4-month period, comments should be made on paper adjacent to each goal regarding success in the area. At that point, new goals should be set for the forthcoming 3 to 4 months. Keep in mind that goals for the summer are relevant. While the emphasis in goals may be more toward personal, social, and family dynamic issues than toward academic achievement, it is important to have a perspective when activities are selected. Many youngsters do need some summer activities to at least maintain their previous year's academic progress and avoid regression.

Long-term goals should be developed and reviewed on an annual basis. Outcome goals are slightly less specific than short-term goals. Remind yourselves of long-term goals when you establish each set of short-term goals. If you find, during any given year, that your youngster has already exceeded his or her long-term goals before the conclusion of the year, then a modification of those long-term goals is appropriate earlier than originally scheduled. If your child has an individual education plan or a Section 504 plan, some of those goals may be adopted and included in your family's long-term annual goals.

MONITORING TREATMENT

▪ It is quite useful to keep notes on various conferences with professionals, particularly teachers, as a permanent record of agreements about future plans. This approach avoids having to rely on your memory of a conversation and allows you to monitor promised interventions for your child. Some parents find it useful to tape record meetings and to complete the form after listening to the tape.

- The importance of regularly scheduled family meetings has been highlighted throughout this book. A record of family meeting notes is also useful, with the notes being read by the entire family after the session. Family agreement on the content of these notes and on decisions precludes many future arguments. This decision-making record can be very helpful when kids protest the agreements. The record indicating their concurrence can be reviewed.

- A diary of treatments should also be maintained. Type of intervention, the professional implementing the intervention, and the short-term goals of the intervention should be recorded. Brief notes can follow as to whether short-term goals have been realized. This record can be quite useful when considering future treatments of a similar nature.

- A diary of medical interventions is extremely valuable. This diary should include the date of initiation, the dosage, the general benefits noted, and the side effects. Such information is very important if further medical trials are necessary with new medications. Medical interventions and your youngster's responses to these medications also represent important data regarding the probable neurotransmitter variation that underlies the youngster's symptoms.

- Active communication with your child's teacher is an extremely important monitoring process. A form completed daily by the teacher and transmitted to you on a weekly basis is the best way to monitor school behavior. An example of this type of form is included in the Appendix. Several principles should be considered. A limited number of target behaviors should be monitored and defined in terms of a positive goal. Negative reinforcement should be avoided. It is important to divide the day into segments so that the student has the maximum opportunity for as much positive feedback as possible. This approach also avoids an excessive reduction in the student's daily score if he or she has only one bad segment. The teacher's observations regarding these behavioral goals should be recorded in a manner that is not embarrassing to the child in the form of undue attention. Discussions with you and your child regarding the process should be conducted in a private, confidential manner.

    Criteria for successfully achieving goals should be carefully defined in collaboration with the student so that he has some sense of ownership of the process and fully understands expectations. It is suggested that the teacher make observations regarding outcome goals each morning, during lunch and recess, and each afternoon. These observations are best recorded at the end of each time segment rather than through recollections at the end of the day or after several days. Behaviors and goals can be modified regularly as the student's responsiveness improves and his or her performance is enhanced.

The full communication form can be sent home with the student at the end of each week, or you can pick it up. Daily report of the number score for that day can allow for regular home rewards. You should develop a reinforcement response to the form before its use is initiated. This menu of rewards should be developed in conjunction with the youngster so that he or she fully understands the benefits of his or her school effort. A timely response is extremely important in order to maintain the interest and involvement of the student. Reinforcers should be available as soon as possible after the report is received. As with most reinforcement programs, the youngster should have the option to accumulate points, chips, and so forth for future larger rewards or reinforcers.

At the early stages of this system, there may be unanticipated problems in completing the form or using the system. Active, ongoing communication between you and the child's teachers will be necessary if the system is to be as smooth and effective as possible.

- Attempt to enhance coordination between all professionals involved in the management of your youngster's ADHD by completing and distributing release of information forms. Also, when contact is made with each professional, be certain that he or she has received information from the others. This intercommunication will enhance the necessary coordination of efforts on the youngster's behalf.

- If possible, identify one professional as the coordinator for the intervention team. This individual, who may be from any professional background, should be willing to take on the responsibility on either a temporary or permanent basis. The coordinator's role can rotate on a regular basis, giving each professional the opportunity to serve. This role does not need to be a highly structured or defined one but can simply ensure that each professional is aware of the strategies being used by the other and guarantee that no contradictory or opposite approaches are being taken.

SPECIFIC INTERVENTIONS

A Time Management Strategy

Many parents find that assisting their youngster in learning time management allows short- and long-term goals to be reached much more readily. This strategy is designed to schedule a youngster's time for afternoons or evenings in collaboration with the youngster. As such, the youngster has a sense of ownership of the schedule and of the allotment of time for various recreational activities, chores, and homework. This strategy also allows visual depiction of time, which can enhance the youngster's concept of time and allow him or her to learn to prioritize activities and responsibilities. Eventually, after regular practice with such strategies, ADHD youngsters will be able to prioritize required activities and time management independently. Forms for this purpose are in the Appendix section.

A Behavioral Management System for Home Responsibilities

The general principles for a behavioral management approach are (a) positive reinforcement, as often as possible, for desired behaviors; (b) avoidance, to the extent possible, of negative responses; (c) recognition of the child's efforts, as well as the products of those efforts; (d) use of personalized rewards; (e) consistency with clearly defined expectations; and (f) expectations that are appropriate for the child's age and developmental status. This approach, and associated rewards, should be developed in conjunction with your child.

The following are the steps involved in creating and implementing a behavioral management approach for compliance with home responsibilities.

1. Even if the idea for a behavioral program originated with the concerns for one child, a similar plan should be adopted for all children in the family at the same time. Each plan should be designed in a manner that is appropriate to the age and development of the particular child. There are several advantages of involving all of the children: avoidance of an excessive focus on the child with ADHD, an opportunity to help the entire family function better, an opportunity to demonstrate the success of the ADHD child to his or her siblings, a decrease in negativity in the family, and a balance for some of the negativity experienced with your ADHD child, as observed by siblings.

2. Select chores and define them specifically. For example, define exactly what "job" has to be done, when it should be completed, and so forth. Your

youngster should be involved in selecting the chores to allow him or her a greater sense of ownership of the process. A maximum of three chores per day should be selected. Chores should involve relatively simple, single-stage responsibilities and should have some relevance to overall household management so that the benefits are real (i.e., taking out the garbage or clearing the table). Teacher feedback regarding school effort or behavior and homework effort can be included as chores. Also, they should fall within the skill level of your child (i.e., they should be chores already completed on an occasional basis). Finally, they should be biased so that there is a high probability of successful compliance; this will enhance the attractiveness of the "new system." Initial successes and rewards will keep the youngster engaged in the process.

3. Compliance should be monitored in a manner that allows for public display of success. A large calendar can serve this purpose. The creation of this calendar should be a family project, everyone pitching in. An example of a calendar is provided in the Appendix. Public display of a youngster's success is important for her or his sense of satisfaction and provides the opportunity for compliments by others. Targeted behaviors should be defined each day, with room allowed for a bonus reinforcer that can be rewarded randomly by you for your child's effort. In addition, an extra line should be available for each day if the youngster takes the initiative to perform an extra task and asks for credit.

4. The criteria for performance of tasks should be clearly defined in terms of both the act and the time frame for completion. The child can indicate compliance within the parameters determined by placing a sticker, star, or checkmark next to the chore assigned on a given day. A noncompliant response should result in you, as the parent, completing the task independently. If your child protests and indicates that she or he was just about to do the task, then simply indicate that you are sure she or he will try harder on the next day. In general, it is not a good idea to remove stars, stickers, or checkmarks already earned. It is important, however, to avoid confrontation when tasks are not completed as expected.

5. Stickers, stars, and checkmarks are reinforcing, but it is best to sustain interest through the provision of something tangible that can gradually accumulate. The use of poker chips can serve this purpose. For each star, sticker, or checkmark, the youngster can be awarded a white poker chip at the end of each day. Accumulation of these tangible objects can be recorded on a form such as the "Reward Bank" found in the Appendix. This Reward Bank statement helps the child keep track of available resources in terms of further rewards. It also can serve as a precaution if chips or play money are lost. Finally, it assists the child in learning mathematics skills, as well as learning the concept of a bank account.

6. Along with your child, develop a list of possible reinforcers or rewards that can accrue with an accumulation of chips. Lists of reinforcers should be accompanied by the cost in chips for each reward. Develop the list with the child and determine the relative value of each task yourselves. If the child protests the cost, be willing to negotiate.

7. It is extremely important that the youngster be allowed to cash in chips or play money regularly. Rules need to be established regarding the cashing in of rewards that involve planning, such as time alone with mom or dad, renting a videotape, or having a friend over. Notice of 24 hours might be required to guarantee these reward options. However, it is acceptable to provide such rewards more spontaneously if adequate arrangements can be made.

8. Modifications of desired rewards and relative costs are often necessary. These adaptations are usually the result of a loss of interest by the youngster in payoffs that have already been achieved regularly. A revision can occur at any time or be scheduled on a 6- or 8-week basis. You as parents can assess the relative costs of the reinforcer whenever changes are made. Again, negotiations may be necessary.

9. When your youngster "cashes in" chips for rewards, her or his interest can be further encouraged by placing the "money" into a long-term reward pool. This larger reward may be a relatively expensive toy or outing. As short-term rewards are purchased, the child continues to accumulate credit toward the bigger item or event. A separate reward bank can be maintained to keep track of this goal. Allowance can be determined by the chips acquired during a given week.

10. The responsibilities or chores being reinforced can also be adjusted over time. Relatively simple chores can be changed to those that are more complicated or require multiple stages to complete. When the original chores are being accomplished regularly, new ones can be added, thus increasing the youngster's opportunity to gain more chips and earn larger rewards. Again, some level of negotiation with the child to maintain her or his sense of ownership is always productive.

TROUBLESHOOTING

Many parents complain that successful reinforcement programs simply lead the child to expect reinforcement for everything he or she does. In fact, when asked to complete a task, some youngsters will immediately respond by negotiating a payoff. Parents often describe feeling resentful under these circumstances and feeling as though the system has backfired, which is not, in fact, the case. Initially, a reinforcement program is most useful when a youngster is noncompliant and, as a result, a negative pattern exists between parent and child. A reinforcement program can reverse this trend. Typically, most youngsters, while enjoying their tangible rewards, benefit most from the positivity in the relationship with their parents as well as their emotional satisfaction with pleasing parents. Asking for reinforcers is a reasonable result of this process. The need for constant reinforcement will gradually disappear. It is important that you not get angry at your child for requesting reinforcement, both because you have taught the child this system and because the ultimate goal is for his or her receipt of your positive attention. It is reasonable, however, once the system is well under way, to ask the youngster to postpone gratification and keep track of successes in a more informal way, thereby reinforcing larger portions of behavior than small defined chores.

Most parents feel most comfortable when they are certain that all steps are being taken on their youngster's behalf and that there is some level of organization to their approach. Using any or all of the suggestions provided here should help you feel organized while maintaining a permanent, accurate history of your child's progress.

Glossary

Achievement tests—Measures of a person's knowledge level in a particular academic subject, such as reading or mathematics. These tests are administered on a one-to-one basis and compared in a large population of individuals of the same gender and similar ages.

Adderall—A new psychostimulant that has not been fully studied in terms of its benefits relative to other medications. It is a combination of four types of amphetamines.

ADHD core symptoms—These symptoms include hyperactivity, inattention, distractibility, impulsivity, and an excessive need for attention.

Adverse effects—Side effects of treatments, particularly medications.

Agitation—Emotional disturbance or excitement; restlessness.

Amitriptyline—A tricyclic antidepressant sometimes used in the treatment of ADHD and depression. The brand name is Elavil.

Amphetamines—A group of stimulant medications used in the treatment of ADHD. These drugs are particularly helpful in the treatment of core ADHD symptoms. Dexedrine is an example. Methamphetamines also fall under this category.

Anafranil—A tricyclic antidepressant. The generic name is clomipramine. This drug is often used in the treatment of obsessive-compulsive disorder.

Anorexia—The loss of appetite.

Anticonvulsant—Medication typically used to treat seizure disorders or epilepsy. Some drugs in this category are used in the treatment of behavioral disturbances.

Antidepressants—Medications that reduce depression and help to elevate mood in a depressed person. Various drugs are included in this category.

Anxiety—A state of being nervous, worried, tense, or stressed. Anxiety disorders coexist with ADHD in about 20% to 25% of individuals. Anxiety may be generalized to all life experiences or may be more specific (for example, as in phobias).

Apraxia—The inability to carry out a complex or skilled movement; not due to paralysis or impaired comprehension.

Articulation—The pronunciation of words.

Auditory discrimination—The ability to discern differences and similarities in what is heard (for example, hearing the words *let* and *lot* as different).

Auditory memory—The ability to recall information that is heard.

Auditory perception—The ability to interpret information that is heard and attribute appropriate meaning to the sounds.

Auditory sequential memory—The ability to remember things that are heard in order, such as a series of directions.

Autism—Spectrum of disorders involving a qualitative disturbance in verbal communication, social interaction, and play or recreational activities.

Aventil—A tricyclic antidepressant occasionally used in the treatment of ADHD. The generic name is nortriptyline.

Behavioral management—A system of interventions designed to change a person's behavior in a desired direction and to discourage undesirable or inappropriate behavior.

Biochemistry—The scientific study of chemical substances and processes of living matter. In regard to ADHD, this term often refers to the interaction of chemicals or neurotransmitters in the nervous system.

Biofeedback—A method of learning to modify a particular body function, such as temperature, blood pressure, or muscle tension, by monitoring it with the aid of an electronic device. Used as a treatment for ADHD and also called "Neurotherapy."

Bipolar disorder—An emotional disorder characterized by periods of mania alternating with depression, often interspersed with relatively long intervals of normal mood.

Blood chemistries—Blood tests that reflect the functioning of various body organs by measuring chemicals in the bloodstream.

Blood levels—Serum concentrations or levels achieved by the administration of medication at various doses. May be useful in determining whether a dose of medication is appropriate or excessive; useful for some drugs but not for others.

Buproprion—An antidepressant medication sometimes used in the treatment of ADHD. The brand name is Wellbutrin.

Caffeine—A stimulant existing in foods. It has been studied as a treatment for ADHD with mixed results.

Chronological age—Real age in years and months. For example, a child who is 7 years, 8 months old would have a chronological age of 7.8. This term is used in interpreting psychoeducational tests.

Clomipramine—A tricyclic antidepressant. The brand name is Anafranil. Often used in the treatment of obsessive-compulsive disorder.

Clonidine—A medication frequently used in the treatment of high blood pressure in both adults and children. It is currently a commonly used medication for the tics associated with tic disorders and Tourette's syndrome. It is also used for the explosive behavior and behavioral negative overreactivity associated with ADHD.

Coaching—The guidance or direction provided by an instructor or a coach. This intervention is frequently used with adolescents and adults to assist them in managing ADHD.

Coexisting condition—A condition that exists simultaneously with another condition. Such conditions exist frequently enough with core ADHD symptoms to be considered as part of the full symptom profile for children, adolescents, and young adults with ADHD.

Comorbid condition—This term is used in scientific literature to describe coexisting conditions.

Compulsive—Characterized by perfectionism, rigidity, conscientiousness, and an obsessive concern with order and detail.

Concentration—Exclusive attention to one object or task; a close mental application.

Conduct disorders—Socially unacceptable behaviors such as stealing, fire setting, truancy, property destruction, robbery or burglary, aggression, physical cruelty to animals, use of a weapon to hurt or intimidate others, and forcing another into sexual activity.

Consequence—The effect, result, or outcome of something occurring earlier. In behavioral management, the term refers to the defined result of or response to a youngster's behavior.

Contraindicated—A term used to indicate that a particular treatment, especially medication, cannot be used in a certain situation.

Coordination—fine/gross—The ability to perform motor tasks in an age-appropriate, effective, and smooth fashion.

Coping—Facing and dealing with adversities and responsibilities, especially calmly and adequately.

Cylert—A stimulant used in the treatment of ADHD. The generic name is pemoline.

Decoding—Converting symbols into understandable concepts (for example, reading words and sounding them out in order to provide meaning).

Depression—A syndrome marked by sadness, pessimism, poor ability to cope with ordinary tasks, lack of enthusiasm, frequent crying, emotional lability, fluctuating mental alertness, and social with-drawal.

Desipramine—A tricyclic antidepressant medication used to treat some individuals with ADHD and depression. The brand name is Norpramin.

Desoxyn—A stimulant drug used in the treatment of ADHD. The generic name is methamphetamine.

Developmental delays—Temporary or permanent delays in the acquisition of a trait or skill such as the ability to walk or talk. Delays are usually defined by the expectations for similar children of the same age and sex.

Dexedrine—A stimulant used to treat ADHD. The generic name is dextroamphetamine.

Dextroamphetamine—A stimulant used to treat ADHD. The brand names are Dexedrine and Adderall.

Disruptive behavioral disorders—A variety of conditions and diagnoses that cause an individual to disrupt usually acceptable social routines in various settings.

Distractibility—A proneness to having attention diverted or drawn away.

Dopamine—A neurotransmitter that allows brain cells to transmit messages for the processing of information. It may be transformed into norepi-nephrine, another neurotransmitter.

Double blind—A research design in which neither the person providing a medication nor the person receiving it knows whether the medication being used is the actual substance or an imitation (placebo). Outcome measures or effects are noted without the awareness of whether the actual substance or a placebo was administered.

Drug holiday—A temporary discontinuation of medical treatment designed to determine the continued presence of medical symptoms and their level of severity without the benefit of medication. Often used to deter-mine the necessity for continued medication and the most appropriate dose.

DSM-IV—The fourth edition of the *Diagnostic and Statistical Manual of Mental Disorders*, published by the American Psychiatric Association. This manual, updated on a periodic basis, contains the diagnostic cri-teria for emotional and behavioral disorders.

Dysarthria—An inability to pronounce words correctly, often resulting from dysfunction in the central nervous system involving the motor coordi-nation of speech.

Dyscalcula—The inability to do simple arithmetic calculations.

Dysfunction—An impairment or malfunctioning, as of an organ or struc-ture of the body.

Dysgraphia—A specific handwriting disability that results in written material being disorganized and illegible.

Dyslexia—The inability to read effectively. May be caused by a variety of neurological, emotional, developmental, and genetic factors; often associated with problems in acquiring writing and spelling skills.

Elavil—A tricyclic antidepressant occasionally used in the treatment of ADHD. The generic name is amitriptyline.

Electrocardiogram—A test that records the electrical impulses generated within the heart. Also called an EKG or ECG. This test is often required as a baseline prior to the use of various medications. The electrocardiogram may be repeated while the individual is on various medications to determine the effect of these medications on electrical or nervous impulses within the heart muscle.

Electroencephalogram—A test, often called a brain wave study, that records the electrical energy created by the brain through multiple leads attached to the scalp. This test is often used when a seizure disorder or epilepsy is suspected. It may also be performed when neurological damage or damage to the brain is suspected.

Emotional—An affective state of consciousness in which moods such as joy, sorrow, and fear are experienced.

Emotional lability—Rapidly changing moods or behavioral expressions of those moods.

Environmental management—Commonly used to describe behavioral management or interventions such as school accommodations used by adults in an effort to assist, direct, and guide a child's or adolescent's behavior and performance.

Expectations—Anticipations of what is reasonable, due, justified, or hopeful for an individual.

Expressive language disorder—An inability to express thoughts in language that is age appropriate. Individuals with this disorder commonly have difficulty with retrieving or finding words, creating full and meaningful sentences, and telling stories in a logical, sequential fashion.

Facilitate—To make easier or less difficult; to help move forward; to assist in the progress of an individual.

Family therapy—A form of counseling or therapy involving family members as a group. The focus is on effective communication between family members and conflict resolution.

Feingold diet—A method of treating ADHD symptoms by limiting or excluding food additives or food colorings.

Fetal alcohol effects—A group of symptoms caused by a mother's consumption of alcohol during pregnancy. These effects typically occur without evidence of any impact on the physical development of the child. In general, the effects on development are less pronounced than those that occur with fetal alcohol syndrome.

Fetal alcohol syndrome—A variety of symptoms and physical abnormalities associated with a mother's consumption of alcohol during pregnancy. The physical symptoms involve facial anomalies or abnormalities, small head size, and growth deficiency. The developmental characteristics may include a variety of developmental delays and academic difficulties, mental retardation, and symptoms often seen in ADHD.

Fluoxetine—A selective serotonin reuptake inhibitor. The brand name is Prozac.

Grade equivalent—The academic skill level of an individual, usually determined by a standardized test administered on a one-to-one basis. A grade equivalent is usually described by the grade and month score for that individual. For example, a child who scores 5.5 in reading would be able to read as well as the average fifth grader in the fifth month of instruction for that school year.

Guilles de la Tourette syndrome—A chronic, hereditary neurological disturbance with motor tics and vocal tics in association with behavioral disturbances such as symptoms of obsessive-compulsive disorder, over-anxiety, unusual fears and phobias, major behavioral outbursts, and attention disorder symptoms.

Hyperactivity —Excessive physical activity, sometimes associated with neurological or psychological causes.

Hyperkinesis—An abnormal amount of uncontrolled muscular activity.

Imipramine—A tricyclic antidepressant sometimes used in the treatment of ADHD. The brand name is Tofranil.

Impulsivity—A sudden involuntary inclination prompting an individual to action or speech. A core symptom of ADHD.

Incidence—Rate of occurrence of an event or condition.

Individual education plan—Written plan for students who qualify for special education within a local school district. The plan incorporates the student's strengths and weaknesses, measurable goals and objectives, educational support services, and procedures for evaluating progress. It is developed in a collaborative effort between the parents and school personnel and ideally involves the student at his or her level of understanding.

Insomnia—Difficulty in falling and staying asleep.

Intelligence quotient—A number derived from the administration and interpretation of an intelligence test. Intelligence, in general, reflects the overall ability to learn, integrate, use, and collate information. Some define IQ as what IQ tests measure. Scores on IQ tests are reported numerically, with a score of 100 being average.

Interactional—Responsiveness pattern that allows individuals to communicate, either verbally or behaviorally.

Intervention—A treatment initiated or carried out to improve a specific skill, performance, or behavior.

Learning disability—An inability to learn in an age-appropriate fashion despite adequate ability, as typically measured by intelligence tests. Discrepancies between ability and performance typically are due to an inefficiency or delay in the ability to process information by the nervous system.

Mainstreaming—Placement of a student who is qualified for special education in regular classes on a partial or full-time basis.

Mental age—A score derived by an intelligence test that describes the individual's overall ability to learn, integrate, use, and collate information expressed in an age equivalent. An individual's age would be expressed in a year and month fashion such as 6 years 9 months based on the results of intelligence tests.

Mental retardation—A disorder of multiple causes characterized by varying degrees of subnormality in ability to learn, integrate, collate, and use information. Degree of mental retardation is typically defined by scores on intelligence tests and by the calculated IQ for the individual.

Metabolism—The sum of physical or chemical processes in an organism by which a substance is produced, maintained, or destroyed and by which energy is made available. In discussions of medication, metabolism typically refers to the mechanism and the time required for the medication to be used, broken down, and excreted from the body.

Methamphetamine—A type of stimulant in the amphetamine category. Also known as "speed." The brand name is Desoxyn.

Methylphenidate—A stimulant used in the treatment of ADHD. The brand name is Ritalin.

Minimum brain damage—Initial name for the cluster of symptoms now called ADHD.

Minimum brain dysfunction—Label that replaced minimum brain damage for the symptoms currently described as ADHD. The choice of the word *dysfunction* was an attempt to better describe what occurred within the nervous system of certain individuals who, in fact, did not have evidence of any neurological damage.

Multimodal approach—A combination of various interventions in the treatment of ADHD. These interventions typically involve educational support services, psychological therapies, behavioral management strategies, and medication.

Neurodevelopmental assessment—An examination that includes a variety of tasks measuring fine and gross motor coordination and sensory interpretation. This test is used by some professionals as an important part of an evaluation for ADHD. Performance on the various tasks involved in this test is compared with that of youngsters of the same gender and comparable ages.

Neurotransmitters—Chemicals produced by nerve cells that travel to adjacent cells, sending impulses along the nerve pathways. Neurotransmitters are often described as being the wiring or circuitry of the brain.

Norepinephrine—A neurotransmitter that has been the focus of interest and investigation for youngsters with ADHD.

Norm—Average or typically expected performance on a given task for any individual. For example, if individuals perform at an average level for their age, they are described as meeting the norm for that age.

Norpramin—A tricyclic antidepressant. The generic name is desipramine.

Nortriptyline—A tricyclic antidepressant. The brand names are Pamelor and Aventil.

Obsessive-compulsive disorder—A condition that involves the persistent intrusion of unwanted thoughts accompanied by ritualistic actions; to be preoccupied with thoughts, feelings, and desires in an intrusive manner. The need for orderliness or sameness. Obsessive-compulsive disorders are part of a broad spectrum of anxiety disorders that may be seen as coexisting symptoms in individuals with ADHD.

Off task—A term that describes an individual who is not adequately paying attention to or participating in ongoing activities.

On task—A term that describes an individual who is paying attention to or participating in an ongoing activity in an appropriate, productive manner.

Overdose—Ingestion of an excessive amount of a medication or substance beyond that which would be prescribed for a given condition. Often used to describe the ingestion of a chemical or medication in an effort to harm oneself in a suicidal gesture or attempt.

Pamelor—A tricyclic antidepressant occasionally used in the treatment of ADHD. The generic name is nortriptyline.

Paroxetine—A selective serotonin reuptake inhibitor. The brand name is Paxil.

Paxil—An antidepressant medication in the selective serotonin reuptake category. The generic name is paroxetine.

Pediatrician—A medical doctor with specialized training in the care of children, adolescents, and young adults up to the age of 21. Most pediatricians are comfortable in the evaluation and initial management of ADHD.

Peer—A person who is the equal of another in terms of abilities, qualifications, age, background, or social status.

Pemoline—A stimulant medication used in the treatment of ADHD. The brand name is Cylert.

Percentile—A number that describes how an individual's score on a test item compares with that of a larger sample population. For example, if someone scored at the 70th percentile, this would mean that 70% of people scored lower and 30% of people scored higher.

Perceptual motor task—An activity requiring coordination of perception (usually visual) and motor movement (such as the skills required for penmanship, artistic activity, athletic skills, or playing a musical instrument while reading music).

Performance—The accomplishment of work or an effort to complete a task.

Placebo—A pharmacologically inactive substance used as a control in testing the effectiveness of a drug or other intervention.

Postsynaptic membrane—The surface of a brain cell receiving an impulse from an adjacent brain cell. These impulses represent the movement of chemicals called neurotransmitters between brain cells.

Presynaptic membrane—The surface of a brain cell from which an impulse originates traveling to an adjacent brain cell. These impulses reflect movement of chemicals between brain cells called neurotransmitters.

Prevalence—The total number of cases of a condition or disorder in a specific location over a certain period of time, often expressed as a percentage. For example, the prevalence of ADHD among school-aged children in the United States is approximately 3% to 6%.

Procrastination—To defer action or to delay until another time.

Production—The act of completing a task or work product.

Prozac—An antidepressant in the selective serotonin reuptake inhibitor category. The generic name is fluoxetine.

Psychiatrist—A medical doctor who specializes in the diagnosis and treatment of emotional and behavioral disorders.

Psychoeducational evaluation—Comprehensive assessment of the skills and abilities relevant to successful accomplishment of educational tasks and learning. These assessments often include an evaluation of youngsters' learning style, academic achievement or knowledge, intelligence level, and emotional factors that may relate to their educational success.

Psychologist—An individual with a graduate degree in the area of psychology that involves the diagnosis and treatment of emotional and behavioral disturbances. Many psychologists are primarily involved in the administration of psychological or psychoeducational testing, while others are involved in counseling or psychotherapy designed to assist individuals in understanding the origin of their feelings and developing effective adaptations of coping strategies.

Rebound—An adverse medication effect that involves an exaggeration of the symptoms under treatment when medical therapy ends. The specific cause of rebound is not known. It is believed, however, that rebound occurs more frequently in individuals in whom the medication leaves the system relatively precipitously or abruptly.

Receptive language processing disorder—A type of learning disability that causes an individual difficulty in understanding or comprehending oral language. The individual may have an adequate attention level and may understand the vocabulary being used but may miss the message being transmitted.

Reinforce—To strengthen the probability of a desired behavior by giving or withholding a reward.

Reinforcer—A response to a behavior that is intended to encourage the behavior or to cause it to extinguish or discontinue.

Remediation—An intervention intended to improve poor skills in a specified area.

Resilience—The ability to recover readily from illness, depression, or adversity.

Resource room—A designated area often used in special education programming for students who qualify for such services. Students are typically pulled from their regular classroom and spend a specified amount of time in the resource room with a limited number of other students. The curriculum within this setting usually focuses on specific areas of weakness that require remediation.

Ritalin—A stimulant medication often used in the treatment of ADHD. The generic name is methylphenidate.

Ritual—Any practice or pattern of behavior regularly performed in a set manner; a specific act, such as handwashing, performed to a repetitive degree.

Self-contained room—A location used in special education programming. Students who are placed in this setting have special education programming throughout their entire school day, representing the vast majority of their academic curriculum. Students may remain in this setting for the entire day or have elective or nonacademic classes in a separate location.

Sertraline—An antidepressant drug in the selective serotonin reuptake category. The brand name is Zoloft.

Side effect—A term used to describe undesirable effects of interventions; most often used to describe such effects for medications. See also Adverse effects.

Self-esteem—Personal perception of one's competence and one's ability to be successful in age-appropriate tasks or challenges.

Special education—Educational programs created by federal law to meet the educational needs of individuals who are not able, for a variety of reasons, to learn successfully at their age and grade level. The qualification criteria education are specifically defined, The services are individualized to the specific needs of each individual student.

Stamina—The strength or power to endure fatigue, stress, and so forth. In the context of the ADHD model described, it defines the physical health, nutrition, energy level, and absence of chronic diseases for an individual.

Stimulant—A drug or other agent that temporarily quickens a vital process or the functional activity of an organ or part.

Stimulus—A sensory experience from one's environment that provokes a response. The sensation may be visual, auditory, or tactile (touch), or it may affect other sensory organs.

Strategy—A plan or method for achieving a specific goal.

Structure—To define the organizational aspects of a situation or the systematic approach to completion of a task.

Support group—A meeting of individuals or the family members of individuals that have a specific diagnosis or condition. Support groups are generally led by professionals who have skills in enhancing effective communication between individuals and who have knowledge of the specific condition that brings a group together. The purposes of most support groups are to obtain knowledge and information about a specific condition, share experiences, and provide emotional support.

Symptomatology—The collective symptoms of an individual or a disease process.

Syndrome—A group of symptoms that, together, are characteristic of a specific disorder, disease, or the like.

Syntax—Study of the pattern of formation of sentences or phrases from words and of the rules for the formation of grammatical sentences within a language.

Temperament—A scientific term used to describe characteristics that often define an individual's personality. An individual's temperament reflects behavioral style rather than content. Temperamental characteristics are viewed as being biologically determined.

Tic—A sudden spasmodic, painless, involuntary muscular contraction, as of the face. Tics may be motor or vocal in nature. Examples of motor tics would be eye blinking, facial grimacing, head shakes, and shoulder shakes. Examples of vocal tics would be grunting, snorting, and swallowing and sniffing involuntarily.

Tic disorder—A disorder highlighted by sudden spasmodic, painless, involuntary muscle contractions and a variety of behavioral disturbances.

Time out—A behavioral management strategy generally in response to an inappropriate or undesirable behavior. The individual is placed in a situation in which interaction with other individuals is not possible. Time-out strategies are often used as punishments. However, the major goal of time out is to provide an opportunity for an individual to regain self-control so that he or she can return to interact more appropriately with others.

Tofranil—A tricyclic antidepressant medication used to treat depression and ADHD. The generic name is imipramine.

Tolerance—A term often used to describe the lack of effectiveness of medical treatment after an individual has been on that treatment for some period of time.

Tourette's syndrome—See Guilles de la Tourette syndrome.

Trauma—Psychological distress resulting from life events outside the range of usual experience, especially if the distress causes a disturbance in normal functioning.

Tricyclic antidepressants—A category of antidepressant medications that share similar chemical characteristics. These drugs are used for depression, and several are used in treating ADHD.

Tutor—A person employed to instruct another, especially privately; a coach.

Underachievement—To perform below the potential indicated by tests of one's mental ability or aptitude. Underachievement can occur for a variety of reasons, including developmental reasons, emotional reasons, and social and cultural reasons.

Visual memory—The ability to recall information that is seen (such as the ability to copy designs after observing them).

Visual perception—The ability to interpret information that is seen and to give it meaning.

Visual perceptual motor disorder—A disorder in which an individual is not able to appropriately perceive visual stimuli so as to effectively respond with an appropriate motor action. For example, reversal of letters when writing or reversal of letters within a word would be a visual perceptual motor disturbance.

Wellbutrin—An antidepressant medication. The generic name is buproprion.

Withdrawal symptoms—Symptoms that occur as medication wears off. Most often used to describe symptoms that occur when a medication is stopped suddenly. May also occur at the end of each dose of a short-acting medication.

Zoloft—An antidepressant in the selective serotonin reuptake category. The generic name is sertraline.

Information Resources

BOOKS FOR PARENTS

Taking Charge of ADHD: The Complete, Authoritative Guide for Parents. Russell A. Barkley

Dr. Barkley empowers parents by arming them with up-to-date information, expert advice, and self-confidence. The book features pioneering research, new insights into preventing ADHD from becoming a major obstacle, step-by-step methods for managing a child with ADHD, the latest information on medications, techniques for enhancing school performance, and a section devoted to parents' needs.

Attention Deficit Disorder: A Parent's Guide. M. Cohen, M. Grynkewich, L. Jaffe, R. Mora, M. Nahmias, G. Powers, R. Daly-Rooney, and J. Schorsch. Tucson, AZ: Arizona Council for Children with Attention Deficit Disorders, P.O. Box 36132, Tucson, AZ 85740.

This manual provides an approach to parental self-education and the evaluation of a child with possible ADHD. Intervention strategies and the roles of various professionals are discussed.

Attention Please: ADHD/ADD. A Comprehensive Guide for Successfully Parenting Children with Attention Disorder and Hyperactivity. Edna Copeland and Valerie L. Love

This book provides a broad overview of ADHD in children and adolescents. The authors have developed several aids to the parental role in evaluation and management. An in-depth approach to comprehensive management is presented.

189

Maybe You Know My Kid: A Parent's Guide to Identifying, Understanding, and Helping Your Child With Attention-Deficit Hyperactivity Disorder. M. C. Fowler

One of the few books for parents on the subject of ADHD written by a parent, and one of the best. The author has become a lay expert on the subject of ADHD through her extensive work on the national level with CHADD.

Why Won't My Child Pay Attention? S. Goldstein and M. Goldstein

A well-written, informative book for parents on hyperactivity (ADHD) and its management by two clinical experts on the subject. They draw on their extensive experience in evaluating and treating ADHD children and adolescents, as well as educating patients and their parents.

Attention Deficit Disorder and Learning Disabilities: Realities, Myths, and Controversial Treatments. B. Ingersoll and M. Goldstein

The best book for parents reviewing the unproven and disproven remedies offered for treatment of children with ADHD; very helpful in sorting out the shams, fakeries, and other quack remedies for ADHD. Also provides a short review of the most useful and scientifically substantiated treatments for ADHD.

A Sourcebook for Managing Attention Disorders: For Early Childhood Professionals. C. B. Jones. Tucson, AZ: Communication Skill Builders.

This is a useful workbook with various exercises and activities that promote attention and task completion skills for teachers and parents.

Why Johnny Can't Concentrate. Robert A. Moss and Helen Huff Dunlap

An excellent overview for parents with practical, time-proven intervention recommendations.

The ADD Hyperactivity Workbook for Parents, Teachers, and Kids. H. Parker

This is a highly useful workbook containing numerous strategies for working with children with ADHD at home and in school. These approaches are considered traditional because they have been time tested and found to be predictably successful.

Dr. Larry Silver's Advice to Parents on Attention-Deficit Hyperactivity Disorder. L. Silver

A nicely written book for parents covering most of the major issues related to ADHD on which parents need information. It provides accurate, timely, sensitive, and practical information on ADHD. The sections on nontraditional therapies are especially useful.

Helping Your Hyperactive Child. John F. Taylor

A comprehensive guide for ADHD, covering identification of effective treatments, development of discipline and self-esteem, and assistance with family adjustment. It includes study questions for group discussions and recent research findings on the causes of ADHD and drug abuse indicators in ADHD adolescents.

Teenagers with ADD: A Parent's Guide. Chris A. Zeigler Dendy

This book takes a comprehensive look at the special issues and challenges faced by ADHD teens, their families, teachers, and treatment professionals. The author discusses all forms of ADD and describes the interaction between these symptoms and adolescent emotional development.

BOOKS FOR CHILDREN AND ADOLESCENTS WITH ADHD

I Would If I Could: A Teenager's Guide to ADHD/Hyperactivity. Michael Gordon

This is a readable, enjoyable, and meaningful book for ADHD teenagers. It allows them to gain an understanding of ADHD and avoids their resistance to discussions about the topic. The information provided is accurate, comprehensive, and presented in a relevant attractive style.

Adolescents and ADD: Gaining the Advantage. Patricia O. Quinn

This book is designed to help students diagnosed with ADD better adjust to the new challenges facing them as they enter middle or high school. The book is filled with valuable advice from doctors, teachers, and, most important, other students with ADD who have experienced fears, successes, and disappointments.

Otto Learns About His Medicine—A Story About Medication for Hyperactive Children. Matthew Galvin

For ages 4–8. Assists hyperactive children and their families in understanding this disorder, as well as the benefits and side effects of medication used for treatment. Using the metaphor of a car with a "motor that goes too fast" to describe the hyperactive child and the image of a mechanic and the doctor, this story is designed to reduce the anxieties and fears of children who take medication.

Jumping Johnny, Get Back to Work: A Child's Guide to ADHD/Hyperactivity. Michael Gordon

A youngster tells this story about his struggles to achieve and not always meeting with success or acceptance. He tells of his frustrations of trying to not get in trouble both at school and at home. The diagnosis process and school/home modifications are explained. The book is written to help ADHD children learn about their difficulties. Siblings or classmates can also gain understanding.

Shelly, the Hyperactive Turtle. Deborah Moss

This primary-level picture book is good for young children who have just found out they have or may have ADHD. Explanations of ADHD behaviors, diagnosis, and treatment (medicine and therapy) are easy to understand.

Slam Dunk: A Young Boy's Struggle with Attention Deficit Disorder Featuring Commonly Asked Questions about ADD. Roberta Parker and Harvey Parker Harvey.

A boy goes through testing and evaluation to determine whether he has ADD. The book discusses some of the frustrations he has at school and at home. School staffs are presented as caring, approachable people who can help identify problems and modify the educational process so that the child can be successful. The story is simplistic, with blank pages at the ends of some chapters.

Putting on the Brakes. Patricia Quinn and Judith Stern

A young people's guide to understanding ADHD, dealing with the feelings and questions of 8- to 13-year-old children. Suggestions are given to help a child gain control over behaviors. A glossary is provided.

Many Ways to Learn: Young People's Guide to Learning Disabilities. Uzi Ben-Ami and Judith Stern

For ages 8–13. A positive, readable book for youngsters with learning disabilities. It defines learning disabilities, illustrates different types, and explains their cause. The book provides reassurance and describes the sometimes confusing effects of learning disabilities on behavior, performance, and emotions.

ADHD AND THE COLLEGE STUDENT

Survival Guide for College Students with ADD or LD. Kathleen G. Nadeau

This useful guide provides students with the information they need to survive and succeed in the college setting. It will help students choose the right college, assess the services a college offers to LD/ADD students, arrange for extended-time exams, maintain helpful relationships with professors, select an appropriate major, and work with career counselors. Suggestions on how students can help themselves are offered.

ADD and the College Student. Patricia Quinn

An informative text for college students and their parents on surviving in the university environment with ADHD. Practical suggestions for success are provided.

The following are directories of colleges and universities with specialized programs and resources for college students with ADHD and/or learning disabilities.

The College Student with a Learning Disability: A Handbook. Susan Vogel

A handbook about college-related issues, including Section 504, for students with learning disabilities and all college personnel. Call Learning Disability Association at (412) 341-1515.

K & W Guide to Colleges for Learning Disabled.

A state-by-state guide by Marybeth Kravets and Imy Wax (Harper-Collins, New York, 1994).

Peterson's Guide to Colleges with Programs for Students with Learning Disabilities.

A state-by-state guide, 4th edition (Peterson's Guides, 1994).

SchoolSearch Guide to Colleges with Programs or Services for Students with Learning Disabilities.

A state-by-state guide by Midge Lipkin (SchoolSearch Press, 1994). Telephone: (617) 489-5784.

Unlocking Potential: College and Other Choices for Learning Disabled People: A Step-by-Step Guide. Barbara Scheiber

A book that assists the reader through the postsecondary selection process. Call Woodbine House at (800) 843-7323.

ADULTS WITH ADHD

Driven to Distraction. Edward M. Hallowell and John J. Ratey

A bestseller on adult ADHD written by two psychiatrists who are ADHD adults themselves. Well-written, thoughtful, and filled with numerous informative case vignettes from their adult clients with ADHD, as well as many useful tips on coping with the disorder.

Answers to Distraction. Edward M. Hallowell and John J. Ratey

The authors of the best-selling book *Driven to Distraction* respond to the most frequently asked questions about attention deficit disorder in this "user's guide" to ADD.

You Mean I'm Not Lazy, Stupid, or Crazy?! K. Kelly and P. Ramundo

A nice addition to the literature on adult ADHD, providing numerous helpful suggestions for recognizing and dealing with the disorder.

PERIODICALS

ADDendum: Newsletter for Adults with ADHD, edited by P. Jaffee. Box 296, Scarborough, NY 10510; telephone: (914) 941-2661.

A newsletter for adults with ADHD prepared by adults with ADHD and containing personal perspectives, useful advice, reviews of available materials and resources, and discussions of controversial topics related to ADHD in adults.

The ADHD Report, edited by R. A. Barkley, The Guilford Press, 72 Spring St., New York, NY 10012; telephone: (800) 365-7006.

The only newsletter specifically dedicated to practicing clinicians who want to remain current on the extensive and rapidly changing scientific and clinical literature on ADHD. Parents of children with ADHD and adults with ADHD may also find the contents useful for staying current on controversial issues and research reports.

Attention! CHADD, 449 N.W. 70th Ave., Suite 208, Plantation, FL 33317; telephone: (305) 587-3700.

A flashy, entertaining, and informative magazine on ADHD, created by the largest national support organization for ADD (CHADD), dedicated to keeping parents and adults informed about the numerous issues related to ADHD.

Brakes: The Interactive Newsletter for Kids with ADD, J. Stern & P. Quinn. Magination Press, 750 First St, N.E., Washington, DC 20002; telephone: (800) 374-2721.

The only newsletter dedicated specifically to children and early adolescents with ADHD. Each issue, filled with information and entertaining activities for children, is prepared by two very compassionate writers on the subject.

CHADD Newsletter, CHADD, 449 N.W. 70th Ave., Suite 208, Plantation, FL 33317; telephone: (305) 587-3700.

A newsletter for parents of children with ADHD and adults with ADHD for members of CHADD.

Challenge: A Newsletter on ADHD, edited by J. Conner, P.O. Box 2001, West Newbury, MA 01985; telephone: (508) 462-0495.

RESOURCES FOR TEACHERS

Books

Attention Without Tension: A Teachers' Handbook on Attention Disorders: ADHD and ADD. E. D. Copeland and V. L. Love

This manual for teachers provides an overview of ADHD and various effective interventions. Recommendations are made for practical classroom interventions.

Teaching the Tiger: A Handbook for Individuals Involved in the Education of Students with ADD, Tourette's Syndrome, or Obsessive Compulsive Disorder. Marilyn P. Dornbush and Sheryl K. Pruitt

The reader obtains an in-depth understanding of what living with these conditions and the skills and interventions necessary in providing services for these children in an educational setting. Educational strategies are simply stated but never simplistic. The book is comprehensive, covering everything including legal rights. It is full of practical, step-by-step, positive interventions.

The ADD Hyperactivity Handbook for Schools. H. Parker

This is a richly detailed book for school psychologists, administrators, and educators on useful approaches to the recognition, evaluation, and management of ADHD within the school setting.

How to Reach and Teach ADD/ADHD Children: Classroom-Tested Techniques and Practical Know-How for Helping ADHD Students. Sandra R. Rief

This comprehensive resource addresses the "whole child" and a team approach to meeting the needs of students with ADHD. Proven, effective strategies to assist students in organizational and study skills are described. A powerful story by a parent of three children with this disorder and interviews with teens and adults provide insight into ADHD.

Videotapes

ADHD in the Classroom: Strategies for Teachers. Russell A. Barkley

An excellent staff training tool, this video program helps teachers to better understand ADHD and equips them to meet the difficult challenge of creating an educational environment that addresses the needs of the ADHD child without neglecting other students. The program provides hands-on demonstrations of useful educational and behavioral techniques for the classroom.

Educating Inattentive Children. Sam Goldstein and Michael Goldstein

This video provides an excellent overview of ADHD for teachers, with practical recommendations regarding management.

VIDEOTAPES FOR PARENTS AND YOUNGSTERS WITH ADHD

ADHD—What Do We Know? Russell A. Barkley

This videotape presents an up-to-date picture of what causes the disorder and how it manifests itself. Dr. Barkley covers the various models of treatment, and the topic is brought to life with actual footage of hyperactive children and interviews with their parents and teachers.

ADHD—What Can We Do? Russell A. Barkley

This second videotape concentrates on management strategies for parents to use at home and for teachers to use in the classroom. The tape provides the best hands-on demonstration available of techniques that have been shown to be effective with ADHD children.

Dr. Barkley's videotapes can be obtained through Guilford Publications, 72 Spring Street, New York, NY 10012; Telephone: (800) 365-7006.

Why Won't My Child Pay Attention? Sam Goldstein

Dr. Goldstein, a knowledgeable and entertaining speaker, provides an easy-to-follow explanation concerning the effect that ADHD has on children at school, home, and in the community. He also offers guidelines to help parents successfully and happily manage the problems these behaviors can cause.

It's Just an Attention Disorder. Sam Goldstein

This videotape is intended for older children and teens with ADHD. It has a fast-paced format and uses comments from teens with ADHD about coping with their disorder.

Dr. Goldstein's tapes can be obtained through the Neurology, Learning and Behavior Center, 670 East 3900 South #100, Salt Lake City, UT 84107; Telephone: (801) 532-1484.

VIDEOTAPES FOR ADULTS WITH ADHD

ADHD in Adults. Russell Barkley

This video provides an informed understanding of the impact of ADHD on adult functioning. An overview of treatment choices is presented.

ORGANIZATIONS

Adult Learning Disabilities Association
510 West Hastings Street, Suite 1322
Vancouver, British Columbia, Canada V6B1L8
(604) 683-5554
FAX: (604) 683-2380

Children with Attention Deficit Disorders (CHADD)
499 N.W. 70th Avenue, Suite 308
Plantation, FL 33317
(305) 587-3700
FAX: (305) 587-4599

Council for Exceptional Children
Division for Learning Disabilities
1920 Association Drive
Reston, VA 22091
(703) 620-3660
FAX: (703) 264-9494

Learning Disabilities Association of America (LDA)
4156 Library Road
Pittsburgh, PA 15234
(412) 341-1515
(412) 341-8077

National Attention Deficit Disorder Association (NADDA)
P.O. Box 488
West Newbury, MA 01985
(800) 487-2282
(508) 462-0495

National Association for the Education of Young Children
1509 16th Street, NW
Washington, DC 20036
(202) 232-8777

National Center for Learning Disabilities (NCLD)
381 Park Avenue South
New York, NY 10016
(212) 545-7510
FAX: (212) 545-9665

Tourette Syndrome Association
800 Compton Road
#14 Lower
Cincinnati, OH 45231

GOVERNMENT AGENCIES

Office of Civil Rights
U.S. Department of Education
400 Maryland Avenue, SW
Washington, DC 20202-4135
(202) 401-3020

Contact OCR with issues pertaining to Section 504 of the Rehabilitation Act (1973) and the Individuals with Disabilities Education Act (IDEA), both of which provide guidelines for the rights of individuals with ADHD in public school settings.

Appendix

1. Parental Self Education
   Major Points Learned
   Questions/Answers

2. Evaluation Records

3. Goal Setting
   Short-Term Goals
   Long-Term Goals

4. Monitoring Treatment
   School Staffing Summary
   Notes of Family Meetings
   Intervention Log
   Medication Diary
   Parent-Teacher Communication Form

5. Specific Interventions
   A Time Management Strategy
     Directions
     Clock Format
   A Behavior Management System
     Calendar
     Reward Bank
     Reward Menu

Readers are invited to reproduce these forms for their personal use.

ATTENTION-DEFICIT/HYPERACTIVITY DISORDER
MAJOR POINTS LEARNED FROM SELF EDUCATION

Date	Major Information Learned	Resource
Example: 12/29/95	40–50% of ADHD kids have learning disabilities	*The Attention Zone*—Cohen

ATTENTION-DEFICIT/HYPERACTIVITY DISORDER
MAJOR POINTS LEARNED FROM SELF EDUCATION

Date	Major Information Learned	Resource

ATTENTION-DEFICIT/HYPERACTIVITY DISORDER
SELF EDUCATION/QUESTION

Date	Question	Answer
Example: 4/12/96	Do ADHD kids have sleep problems?	Yes—45% suffer from all types, especially falling asleep.

ATTENTION-DEFICIT/HYPERACTIVITY DISORDER
SELF EDUCATION/QUESTION

Date	Question	Answer

ATTENTION-DEFICIT/HYPERACTIVITY DISORDER
EVALUATION RECORD

Date of Evaluation	Name of Facility	Name of Professional	Major Findings	Location of Report
Example: 10/17/95	Attention Disorder Center	Michael Cohen, M.D.	1. Probable ADHD 2. Fine motor coordination problem 3. Adjustment Reaction with loss of self-esteem	4713 N. First Avenue Tucson, AZ 85718 (520) 887-1438

ATTENTION-DEFICIT/HYPERACTIVITY DISORDER
EVALUATION RECORD

Date of Evaluation	Name of Facility	Name of Professional	Major Findings	Location of Report

ATTENTION-DEFICIT/HYPERACTIVITY DISORDER
SHORT-TERM GOALS (3-4 MONTHS)

Date	Area	Goals	Review Date	Outcome	Lessons to be learned
Example: 2/14/96	Social	Have classmate over to play for 3 hours without incident	5/29/96	Too long—change to 2 hours	Must adjust expectations to his level of comfort
	Family interaction	Clear dinner table cooperatively		Continue effort. Does better if working with someone	Does chores best if working with someone instead of alone
	Academic	Redesign approach to homework		Two sessions 15 minutes each with break between is best	Gets almost as much work done when he knows he'll be done soon
	Other Intervention	Improve attitude about tutoring		Tutors best before dinner	Needs a break after school, evening too late
	Other area				

ATTENTION-DEFICIT/HYPERACTIVITY DISORDER
SHORT-TERM GOALS (3-4 MONTHS)

Date	Area	Goals	Review Date	Outcome	Lessons to be learned

ATTENTION-DEFICIT/HYPERACTIVITY DISORDER
LONG-TERM GOALS (1 YEAR)

Date	Area	Goals	Review Date	Outcome	Lessons to be learned
Example 8/15/95	Social	Gradual improvement in social skills in order to participate in Cub Scout overnight and regular activities.	8/15/96	Has had 3 months of activities without incident. Got 3 merit badges. Overnight in September— Ready!	Collaboration with Scout leader essential.
	Family Interaction	Decrease fighting with sister by 50%. Complete designated 3 chores daily. "Successful" vacation.		Fighting with sister continues but more at a "normal level." Completing chores at approx. a 90% level. No more struggling about chores. "Great" vacation.	Structured positive reinforcement makes huge difference. Design a vacation with slower pace.
	Academic	No D's on report card. Increased completion of work. Tutoring should assist learning process and reduce struggles with parents over homework.		Skills continue to advance nicely. Performance up. Grades much better with accommodations. Tutoring tolerated well before dinner. Much fewer homework struggles.	He will need accommodations from the beginning of every year. Meeting with him and the teacher early in year helps.
	Other Interventions	Martial arts scheduled to improve control and self-esteem.		He loves it. Very motivated. Reaches goals regularly.	Individual rather than team sports are best.
	Other Areas				

ATTENTION-DEFICIT/HYPERACTIVITY DISORDER
LONG-TERM GOALS (1 YEAR)

Date	Area	Goals	Review Date	Outcome	Lessons to be learned

ATTENTION-DEFICIT/HYPERACTIVITY DISORDER
SCHOOL STAFFING SUMMARY

Date	Attendees	Positive Observations	Concerns	Accommodation Decisions	Review Date
Example: 1/22/96	Parents Science teacher Math teacher English teacher School counselor	1. More participation in class 2. Less talking to friends in class 3. Accepts teachers' directions better	1. Not turning in homework 2. Excessive homework because of incomplete classwork 3. Does not complete tests in time allowed	1. Reduction in the volume of work. Give full credit for completed work 2. Allow student to complete classwork and test in a quiet, nondistracting location 3. One hour 15 minutes max. homework each night. Full credit for completed work	3/25/96

ATTENTION-DEFICIT/HYPERACTIVITY DISORDER
SCHOOL STAFFING SUMMARY

Date	Attendees	Positive Observations	Concerns	Accommodation Decisions	Review Date

ATTENTION-DEFICIT/HYPERACTIVITY DISORDER
NOTES OF FAMILY MEETINGS

Date	Notes	Initials of members who agree
Example: 1/15/96	All family members will help clean up kitchen after dinner before starting other activities. The chores are: 1. Clear table 2. Clean and put dishes in dishwasher 3. Clean stove, sink 4. Sweep floor 5. Put leftovers away Mom or dad will make up schedule for two weeks at a time to assign jobs.	_____ _____ _____ _____ _____ _____ _____ _____

ATTENTION-DEFICIT/HYPERACTIVITY DISORDER
NOTES OF FAMILY MEETINGS

Date	Notes	Initials of members who agree

ATTENTION-DEFICIT/HYPERACTIVITY DISORDER
INTERVENTION LOG

Beginning Date	Type of Intervention	Frequency of visits	Name and Address of Professional	Techniques Strategies	Ending Date	Benefits Noted
Example: 12/6/95	Learning Strategies	every 2 weeks	Jane Doe, M.Ed. 5061 E. 5th St. Tucson, AZ 85711 520-529-1628	1. Making outlines 2. Time management 3. Test preparation 4. Steps in writing essay	4/8/96	Improved efficiency and organized approach to learning—very helpful

ATTENTION-DEFICIT/HYPERACTIVITY DISORDER
INTERVENTION LOG

Beginning Date	Type of Intervention	Frequency of visits	Name and Address of Professional	Techniques Strategies	Ending Date	Benefits Noted

ATTENTION-DEFICIT/HYPERACTIVITY DISORDER
MEDICATION DIARY

Beginning Date	Medication	Maximum Dose	Target Symptoms	Benefits	Side Effects	Stop Date	Reason for Stopping
Example: 9/16/95	Ritalin	10 mg AM 10 mg noon 5 mg after school	1. Hyperactivity 2. Inattention 3. Impulsivity	1. Dramatic improvement 2. Inconsistently better 3. Minimal change	Major loss of appetite Stomachache	11/14/95	Weight loss of 7 pounds

ATTENTION-DEFICIT/HYPERACTIVITY DISORDER
MEDICATION DIARY

Beginning Date	Medication	Maximum Dose	Target Symptoms	Benefits	Side Effects	Stop Date	Reason for Stopping

ATTENTION-DEFICIT/HYPERACTIVITY DISORDER
PARENT-TEACHER COMMUNICATION FORM

Name _____

Teacher _____   Week of _____

L/R = Lunch/Recess

Behavior / Goal	Monday AM	Monday L/R	Monday PM	Tuesday AM	Tuesday L/R	Tuesday PM	Wednesday AM	Wednesday L/R	Wednesday PM	Thursday AM	Thursday L/R	Thursday PM	Friday AM	Friday L/R	Friday PM
Behavior—Work completion															
Goal—To be complete and hand in work in time allotted	4	NA	2	2		1	5		4	2		2	5		3
Behavior—Wait for turn															
Goal—Raise hand and wait to be called upon before answering	3	NA	2	3		2	3		2	2		2	4		3
Behavior—Allow others to do their work															
Goal—Stay in own desk quietly during work periods	5	NA	3	5		3	4		1	3		1	5		2
Behavior—Follow playground rules															
Goal—Wait for turn to use swings, slide or sandbox	NA	2	NA		4			5			2			4	
Effort to Achieve Goals	4			3			5			2			4		

Rating Scale: 1 - Unacceptable 2 - Marginal 3 - Improved 4 - Good 5 - Excellent

	Monday	Tuesday	Wednesday	Thursday	Friday
Total Points	25	23	29	18	30

Total Week | 125

ATTENTION-DEFICIT/HYPERACTIVITY DISORDER
PARENT-TEACHER COMMUNICATION FORM

Name _____

Teacher _____

Week of _____

L/R = Lunch/Recess

	Monday AM L/R PM	Tuesday AM L/R PM	Wednesday AM L/R PM	Thursday AM L/R PM	Friday AM L/R PM
Behavior					
Goal					
Behavior					
Goal					
Behavior					
Goal					
Behavior					
Goal					
Effort to Achieve Goals					

Rating Scale: 1 - Unacceptable   2 - Marginal   3 - Improved   4 - Good   5 - Excellent

	Monday	Tuesday	Wednesday	Thursday	Friday
Total Points					

Total Week

ATTENTION-DEFICIT/HYPERACTIVITY DISORDER TIME MANAGEMENT STRATEGY DIRECTIONS

1. Draw a circle for each available hour during the time period to be scheduled.

2. Divide the circles into quarters for each 15-minute period.

3. Set the necessary ground rules (i.e., homework must be completed by such-and-such a time, or a maximum of 30 minutes of TV or computer game time).

4. List the desired and required activities to be completed or enjoyed.

5. Review the list and decide priorities (i.e., what's most important in order 1, 2, 3, 4, etc.).

6. Fill in the circles in priority order.

7. Post the schedule where it is visible to the youngster throughout the time period.

8. Provide reminders at transition times. If this cuing is met with resistance, remind the youngster that he determined his schedule and that he'll have a chance to change his schedule for the next day if he wants to.

Attention Deficit Hyperactivity Disorder
Time Management Strategy
Example

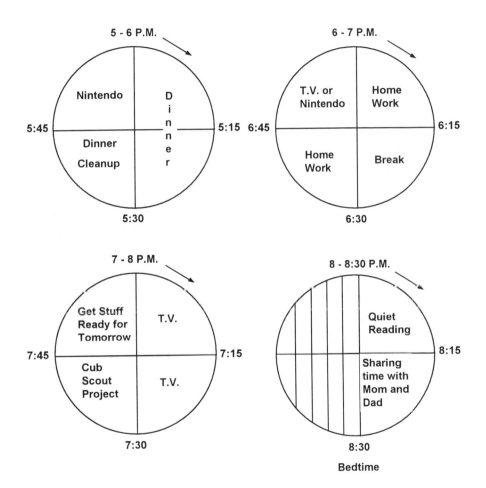

5 - 6 P.M.

Nintendo | Dinner
5:45 | 5:15
Dinner Cleanup | Dinner
5:30

6 - 7 P.M.

T.V. or Nintendo | Home Work
6:45 | 6:15
Home Work | Break
6:30

7 - 8 P.M.

Get Stuff Ready for Tomorrow | T.V.
7:45 | 7:15
Cub Scout Project | T.V.
7:30

8 - 8:30 P.M.

Quiet Reading
8:15
Sharing time with Mom and Dad
8:30
Bedtime

Attention Deficit Hyperactivity Disorder
Time Management Strategy

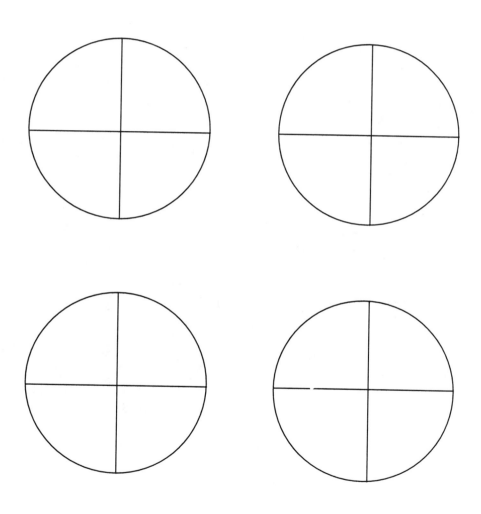

ATTENTION-DEFICIT/HYPERACTIVITY DISORDER
BEHAVIOR MANAGEMENT APPROACH—CALENDAR

	1	2	3	4	5
6	7	8	9	10	11	12
13	14	15	16	17	18	19
20	21	22	23	24	25	26
27	28	29	30	31		

9

Chore
1
2
3
Bonus
Extra Credit

9

Chore
1 - Take out garbage   *
2 - Clear dinner table   *
3 - Feed cat   *
Bonus
Extra Credit

ATTENTION-DEFICIT/HYPERACTIVITY DISORDER
REWARD BANK

Date	Deposit (Add)	Spent (Take away)	Balance (# left)
5/1/96	+3		3
5/2/96	+4		7
5/3/96	+3		10
5/4/96	+4	-4	10
5/6/96	+3		13
5/7/96	+3	-7	9
5/8/96	+2		11
5/9/96	+3		13
5/10/96	+4		17
5/11/96	+3	-6	14
5/12/96	+2	-4	12
5/13/96	+3	-10	5
5/14/96	+3		8
5/15/96	+3		11
5/16/96	+5		16

ATTENTION-DEFICIT/HYPERACTIVITY DISORDER
REWARD BANK

Date	Deposit (Add)	Spent (Take away)	Balance (# Left)

ATTENTION-DEFICIT/HYPERACTIVITY DISORDER
REWARD MENU

Reward	Cost
Example Video game—30 minutes	4 white chips
TV time—30 minutes	4 white chips
Special time with mom	7 white chips
Special time with dad	7 white chips
$2.50 towards toy	10 white chips
$5.00 towards toy	15 white chips
Rent home video movie	6 white chips
Go to movie with friend	5 white chips (we pay admission)
Stay up extra one hour—weekend	8 white chips

ATTENTION-DEFICIT/HYPERACTIVITY DISORDER
REWARD MENU

Reward	Cost

Index